To Ladybug,
May Magic B
Your Guide!

With Love,
Bilal
10.10.23

ii

# *Magic Flight*
# *A Story of Bliss Reborn*

*By Brian Black*

### Brian Black's

### *Magic Flight: A Story of Bliss Reborn*

*An Inner Sky Book*

This book may not be reproduced in whole or part, in any form, without the written permission of the author. Except for brief quotations in articles.

For more information visit  brianjblack.com

This book is based upon real – life experiences

**Original Copyright © 2007 Brian Black**

**Revision Copyright © 2009 Brian Black**

ISBN 978-0-578-01910-9

## *Acknowledgement*

*This book is dedicated to all the dispellers of darkness that have come into my life; without them, there is no way this book would exist.*

*To everyone who helped with this book, especially Kim, Jenny, Maggie and Stephanie. To my parents, all my love and thanks. To my brothers who gave me so much fodder and to my childhood friends, the souls with whom I arrived on planet earth for some reason.*

*To my children, Matt and Becky who helped me keep my own child alive, words can never describe my love for you both.*

*And, most of all, to the Divine in all of us.*

*Without that, nothing would be worth writing about!*

*"This World In Which You Seem To Live, Is Not Your Home.*

*Somewhere Deep Inside, You Know That This Is The Truth."*

*-- A Course In Miracles*

*"I Think, Therefore, I am ... Unconscious."*

*-- Sahdguru Jaggi Vasudev*

*This is not a child's book.*

*Then again, it is.*

*It is for the child in you that has fallen asleep. The one who came into this world full of life and replete with joy.*

*"Magic Flight; a Story of Bliss Reborn" is about a young boy who sees a magician one day, and decides to become one.*

*Ironically, however, the world doesn't stay magic when adulthood arrives and Dougie Whitestone has achieved the heights of "success" as a "professional" magician.*

*Despair leads the boy-turned-man to the brink of self-destruction and that's when the magic reappears, bigger and better than ever...*

*So enter a magical world today in this charming yet challenging, profound yet wonderfully succinct book written by author Brian Black.*

# Content

| | |
|---|---|
| Acknowledgements | iii |
| Prologue: Perspective | 1 |
| Chapter I: the Announcement | 4 |
| Chapter II: the Trip | 10 |
| Chapter III: Nighthawk! | 13 |
| Chapter IV: Almost Christmas | 25 |
| Chapter V: Christmas Eve | 31 |
| Chapter VI: Christmas! | 39 |
| Chapter VII: the Next Day | 51 |
| Chapter vii.5 | 56 |
| Chapter VIII: Splintering | 57 |
| Chapter IX: Grown Up? | 65 |
| Chapter X: Goodbye | 77 |
| Chapter XI: Flight | 81 |
| Chapter XII: The Void | 83 |
| Chapter XIII: Magic Flight | 120 |
| Chapter XIV: I'm Back | 133 |
| Chapter XV: Once Again | 135 |

## PERSPECTIVE.

The last time I left my body it was like taking off an old pair of boots that had been way too tight … for way too long!

Once I was free of that heap of dirt, I exploded into the ionosphere and began jetting around like lightning: zigging in this direction then zagging in that. As soon as I was done lugging around that bag of sand and water for seventy-five earth-years, it felt *so* good when I got free of it that I thought I might want to spend all of eternity just zipping around like a wild and untamed rocket ship. Never again would I allow myself to be saddled with such a slug-like apparatus.

But, on second thought, you never know.

I mean, I don't have to. I don't have to be "human" again. I don't *need* to.

I'm done.

The fruit finally ripened and off I fell! Thank God.

Now, however, I am here again, but in a different capacity. Now I am what many of you call an "angel." In actuality, there is no such thing as an angel; there are only other versions of your Self, your beautiful, wonderful, glorious, timeless and boundless Self. But more of that later on! Now I'm here without a physical body in order to help those who have fallen asleep and that is practically everybody, as you have become a race of sleepwalkers.

The nature of this sleep that has overtaken humankind is important to understand, and that is the reason for my telling of this story. People purportedly grow up as they age, but they actually grow down. They forget how to laugh and how to play and how to have fun. They usually become unhappy and miserable. They forget the magic that they knew as children. So this story is for all the "adults" who have forgotten, that they might remember again.

I am now called Juriel, but on my last journey to your planet, my name was Sherwood.

Sherwood B. Nighthawk.

This is the story of someone I knew and mentored in that lifetime, someone who grew very dear to me for his sheer love of magic. So, let us begin when he was eight years old, in a place called Deerfield Township, Michigan, in the earth year known as 1958.

Please, pay close attention, because many of the secrets to waking up are contained herein.

Oh, and by the way, just in case you wanted to know, I won't be interrupting unless it becomes a true imperative to do so.

I truly hope you enjoy the story.

# CHAPTER I: *THE ANNOUNCEMENT*

Little Dougie Whitestone's copper-colored eyes blazed with excitement.

They drank in every bit of light that was bouncing off the spectacle that held him mesmerized. There before him was a glossy three-foot by three-foot black and white poster. It featured the portrait of a distinguished looking gentleman who sported a salt and pepper goatee with a handlebar moustache and a black silk top hat. It was an announcement proclaiming the arrival of the magician, the "Famous Flying Magician," Sherwood B. Nighthawk.

"Nighthawk!" Dougie gasped. "Oh my God, he's coming here!"

"Why would he come here?" queried Tommy Ross, Dougie's eccentric friend who was standing alongside his companion. "He's like famous all over the world! Why would he come to our church?"

"Who cares? All I know is I must see him! It's magic Tommy! Magic! I wonder if Dad'll take me…"

"Ooo God, ya think?" asked Tommy "Can I come too?"

By now, Tommy was talking to the space formerly occupied by his friend's body. And all he saw as he turned around were Dougie's elbows pumping up and down like an Arabian oilrig; he was galloping home.

Tommy was a lanky kid. Even though he was born on the same day as Dougie, by the time they had celebrated their eighth year of life, Tommy was a good two inches taller than Dougie. But he barely outweighed him. Tommy was the only boy in his family with two older sisters who babysat for Dougie. Most of the time he was fun to be around because he seemed to like mischief as much as Dougie. But, as is so often the case with young boys, the two had several fights before they became friends. Tommy had the strange habit of sucking in his cheeks like a squirrel with nuts in his mouth, just before he threw a punch. This turned out to be an enormous help to young Whitestone, who would have been pulverized a lot more often had this clue not been so vividly telegraphed.

But today, none of that mattered.

Puffing and panting after a seven-block sprint, Dougie clambered up the gray cement steps of his front porch and hustled into the house. A quick search of the

Whitestone abode confirmed what he had suspected: nobody home!

He sat down on the small, carpeted step just inside the front door, rested his feet on the blue slate floor of the foyer, and began his vigil.

*Magic, magic, real magic!* Dougie's mind had become a mantra.

Finally, after a wait of some two hours, Dougie heard his Dad's car pull in the drive. He bolted out the door, jumped over the steps like an Olympic hurdler, and screeched to a halt two inches away from the driver's side door blocking his father's egress.

"Dad! Dad! Dad! Can I go see Nighthawk? Will you take me? Huh? Will you Dad? Will you?"

Dougie's heart was pounding while his mind was still intoning *Magic, magic, real-live magic!* It seemed like forever as he waited for his Dad's answer.

Jeremy Whitestone was still thinking about his day at work, tedious and more to do than could ever be done. He was frequently gruff when he first got home but today something made all of that go away as he saw the look in his son's eyes and intuitively recognized it.

He rolled down the window and smiled at Dougie. He knew who Nighthawk was for he too was once a big fan of magic. The answer was easy and so it came.

After he heard the news, Dougie vaulted over the small white fence in the front yard and went bounding back out into the street to tell Tommy.

"Yes!" the lad was shouting, "He said yes! My Dad is so cool Tommy!

He said you could come too! And my cousin Jimmy. Yes, yes, yes! Oh God, I can hardly wait."

Douglas Whitestone was barely five-feet tall and weighed in at an even ninety-eight pounds soaking wet. There was another boy who lived on the same block named Dougie, Dougie Williams. But he was four years older and quite a bit bigger than "Little" Dougie. So, to keep it all straight, most of the neighborhood called the older boy "Big Dougie" and the younger one "Little Dougie." The only ones who didn't call Dougie Whitestone "Little" were the teachers at school and the parish priest. They called him 'Douglas' or 'Mr. Whitestone.' All except Mrs. Udall that is. She called him "Sweetie" and was Dougie's favorite teacher. She was everybody's favorite teacher. Everybody that was a boy, that is. Dougie, along with every other pre-pubescent boy at the school, thought she was *too* fine. She always wore tight skirts and high-heeled pumps. It made them all sweat, even in the winter.

The priest at the church always called him "Douglas John," adding his Confirmation name. He called everyone by his or her "Christian name," as it was "the proper thing to do." And, of course, there were his parents. They too called him "Little Dougie" or just "Dougie", except when they were mad; then it was "Douglas Joseph John Whitestone!"

Little Dougie liked that as much as he liked spam with his eggs and washing behind his ears.

Deerfield Township was a predominantly Irish Catholic, upper middle-class suburb of Detroit, Michigan. After World War II one-and-a-half-story redbrick houses were cloned hundreds of thousands of times and strung together in neat little rows all over America, and Deerfield was no exception. Eventually the dirt roads were paved and curbed as a generation of mature elm and maple trees reached across to one another, forming comforting tunnels of leafy splendor. The place was quiet and peaceful and everybody seemed to know what life was about. Stay out of trouble, be good, work hard. If you were a boy, get a good job, then get married; if a girl, get married to the right boy. Then raise a family of your own and live in a quiet and peaceful place until you retire and eventually die.

Simple. Obvious.

But pretty depressing to anyone who believed in magic.

## CHAPTER II: *THE TRIP!*

Usually, when the kids went somewhere, the task of chauffeuring them around fell on Rosie, Dougie's mom. She drove a dark green, seven-year-old 1951 Ford Victoria that had been given to her by her father a few years into her marriage. She affectionately called it "Ol' Bess".

Little Dougie's father, Jeremy, didn't do as much as he would have liked with his kids because he was a very busy man. He spent most of his time working, either around the office or around the house. But that just served to make tonight's excursion to the church hall extraordinary. So it wasn't every day that you got to go somewhere with Dad, but to go see magic…*real* magic…now that was something. Something special. Something wonderful.

"Spaz!"

"You are a total dufus TW!" growled Little Dougie.

"I'm rubber, you're glue. Whatever you say bounces off me and sticks to you!" retaliated Dougie's older brother Tad, who absolutely loathed being called "TW." The reason for his hatred of that particular moniker was because that's what his mom called him in front of all his friends last summer when he was nine years old. He had just returned home from summer camp when she called him "TW" and kissed him right there in front of all his friends.

*Yecch!* Tad thought as he shivered just remembering that horrid day.

"I can't believe you TW! You fart! You wore my Yankee shirt again! God I hate you!"

Tommy and Jimmy were already waiting in the back seat of Jeremy's brand new beige 1958 Chevy Impala. Earlier they had walked to the Whitestone's house together because they lived next door to one another just a half-block away. Jimmy was a first cousin on Rosie's side of the family and walked freely into the house whenever he wanted, just like one of the Whitestone kids. Everybody loved him and knew he was destined for great things. He was already working on his fifth scout merit badge; that put him three badges ahead of Dougie.

Dougie was still murmuring as Tad strolled pompously out to the car in a genuine cobalt blue New York Yankee game shirt: the victor's spoils.

Dougie threw on his Green Bay Packer sweatshirt, grabbed his Detroit Tiger baseball cap and bolted out the door. By the time he got to the car he'd forgotten the whole thing with Tad. He was going to see *real* magic, and nothing was going to ruin this night.

Nothing.

Not even his sadistic older brother.

They were on their way.

## CHAPTER III: *NIGHTHAWK!*

It was a cool autumn evening. The trees of Deerfield Township had turned into a blazing mixture of rich reds and deep glistening golds; luxuriant leafy grandeur of purple and auburn pulsated in vibrant magnificence. Nearly half of these gloriously-colored shields from the summer heat now breezed across the night air as the rest clung tenaciously to their branches.

"Dad! Look! There! That must be him Dad! Look, look! He's stepping out of a *Limo* Dad. Wow!"

The words "Spectacular Nighthawk" were boldly emblazoned on a twenty-four-carat-gold personalized license plate on the front of a long, shiny black Cadillac.

Dougie noticed that it wasn't a Lincoln. He remembered how his grandpa –"Papa" they called him – always told him that Lincolns were better than Cadillacs. It just so happened Papa owned a Lincoln dealership and always drove a Continental, but that didn't really matter.

Not now...

What mattered most to Dougie was magic. Yes siree. Magic, magic, magic! That's all that mattered because Little Dougie Whitestone's eyes were filled with magic. And because his eyes were filled with magic, that's all he saw. So for him it permeated the entire universe.

Little Dougie watched without breathing as Sherwood B. Nighthawk's paten leather shoes gently landed on the asphalt drive that led to the church hall. His tophat in hand, his cane in the other, the prestidigitator par-excellence seemed to glide over the dark slate porch and disappeared into the waiting doorway of the church's hall.

Dougie's dad pulled his Chevy into a parking space, threw the beige three-speed column gearshift into first gear and clicked on the parking brake. The boys clambered out noisily giggling about some little secret joke Jeremy didn't hear. Off they zipped, nearly falling over each other as they raced to the old portal and tugged with all their might in a rare moment of cooperation to heave the heavy steel door aside. They ran inside, their hearts pounding with anticipation.

"Stop!" came the harsh and penetrating cry.

Their feet froze to the gym floor, motionless like a fleeing convict trapped in the revealing glare of a midnight spotlight.

The cold shrill of Mrs. Kruzetcha's voice scraped like fingernails on a blackboard as her command filled their schoolboy ears with a familiar fear. The brothers were sure she was a witch—not the fifth grade math teacher she pretended to be. And they all hated how she told them to remember her name. "It's missus crusade-cha," she would somberly intone. All school year long!

"Nobody has *orange* hair" they would laugh, "…unless they've been in league with Satan." And then they would laugh some more, as long as they knew she was nowhere near of course. But right now they were frozen like tundra.

"Where are your tickets *boys*?" she asked with a sadistic glee in her prying query. She was sitting behind an eight-foot table that, not accidentally, resembled a border patrol waystation.

"Right here!" Jeremy's masculine voice boomed across the gym. He didn't like her either. She reminded him of his own fifth grade teacher.

"They must've all gone to the same school, the same evil university" he whispered, making sure she didn't hear. The boys unfroze and silently chuckled as Jeremy shuffled his kids past her church-lady checkpoint, tossing the tickets onto the table without so much as a nod to Mrs. Kruzetcha.

"Little dictators" he muttered to the kids' sheer delight. Moments later the vile Mrs. Kruzetcha was completely forgotten as they sat down on metal fold-up chairs with heavily-salted, yellow-larded popcorn and syrupy colas that came from the other eight-foot table in the gym: the much-loved concession stand.

Our Lady of the Stars church hall was the most recent addition to a church-school complex that acted as the veritable core, the central vortex of the lives of the people that lived in this little suburb. This was where they worshipped and prayed. This was where their kids were baptized, received their first communion and eventually got married. This was where they played baseball and basketball and football and, of course, bingo. And this was where they held their funerals and said goodbye to one another at life's end.

At least the Catholic ones.

And as far as they were concerned, they *were* the only ones. Well, the only ones going to heaven anyway. Of course, in truth, they couldn't be too sure of that either.

Not that they were the only ones that thought that way, mind you, but non-Catholics to them were like the "pagan babies" that one could adopt for a nickel a day at the parish school. A pagan baby might make it to limbo or something, but heaven, no way.

Twelve minutes after taking their seats, the crowd began to hush as the lights dimmed. Waiting until the last possible moment, the boys quieted down as well.

An eerie silence filled the hall.

Deep round tones of swelling drumbeats and throbbing shamanic music announced the shows' beginning as the jet-black, fourteen-foot-high stage curtains quietly parted.

A rainbow-colored fog stood upon a low cloud of smoke that dripped over the edge of the stage. It enshrined a figure of such striking femininity that Tad and Jeremy, Tommy and Jimmy all appeared in need of having their jaws wired shut as the curtain finished opening. The magician's svelte assistant oozed with an energy that would make a sailor blush, though Dougie barely noticed. She stood lightly in her nylon flesh-tone stockings, her right knee cocked and her waist narrow and taut, her back smoothly arched. The fingertips of her left hand slid over her shapely hip, up along her side and stretched gently to the sky, introducing "The Famous Flying, The One and The Only, The Spectacular Magician Extraordinaire: Nighthawk!"

    The music boomed with a choice thickness as timpani drums began to pound a rhythm that added to the already delicious sensory feast. The long-awaited magician now arrived. He quickly and silently strolled to center stage. With a deft motion of his right hand and then his left, out of empty space he produced a clinking pair of handcuffs. He lightly glided to the front of the stage where he held them out for the mandatory audience inspection. A young lad in the front row leapt at the opportunity and grabbed the manacles, scrutinized them thoroughly and, convinced of their integrity handed them back. Nighthawk presented them to his charming aide who quickly opened them up and clasped them around the waiting wrists of the smiling magic man. One tug, then a second demonstrated that his hands were thoroughly bound while Monica, his beautiful assistant, and perfect distraction, reached into a black box nearby to produce a twelve-foot rope. She spun it around his torso, tying him firmly from shoulder to ankle where sturdy steel chains were secured with bulletproof chrome padlocks.

Into the murkiness at the back of the stage, she disappeared. Moments later she came back wheeling out an upright box the size of a man. Its gaping darkness swallowed up Nighthawk as Monica slammed it shut with an audible bang. A deafening knock came from within. Then another. And another. Then the enclosure sprang open and out stepped the Spectacular Nighthawk, free of the handcuffs, unfettered by rope and tossing aside the now feeble looking steel chains and their measly padlocks.

The crowd applauded – but Little Dougie – little eight-year-old Dougie – was unable to clap: because he was in a spell! He now looked the way the others appeared when the stage's curtain first lifted to reveal Monica's physique. His jaw dropped, his shoulders slumped forward and his eyes rolled up so far he could see backwards as he gasped in amazement.

His memory took him back almost a year:

It was still snowing and it was still dark at five-thirty in the morning on a crisp winter day. The world was adorned with two inches of pure neon-white perfection as he reached the school grounds on his way to serve as altar boy at the six o'clock mass at Our Lady of the Stars Church. Little Dougie was captured in gleeful awe by the absolute, unadulterated beauty of it all. He knew he had plenty of time before church; but he was about to lose all sense of time as "it" happened.

"It," was a moment.

Just a moment.

A single, solitary moment of such sheer ecstasy, such utter magnificence, that it held the power of life itself. Inside this moment lay the bliss of existence.

And, if that weren't enough, some day this moment would save Dougie's life, for it would be the hingepin, the King of all Moments, the Moment of Moments that would remind him for all time of what he had forgotten.

On that incredible morning Little Dougie Whitestone took a running start and slid across the perfectly white, perfectly untouched, glistening snow of God. Little Dougie Whitestone, beneath a glowing streetlamp, made time stand still and glided straight into Heaven itself.

Somehow, for that One Moment, for that One, Perfect Moment, he knew he was perfect too.

He was a perfect child in a perfect moment in a perfect world. He saw clearly, vividly, without distortion.

He was truly in touch with the magic.

No, he *was* the magic.

And it would never leave him.

Oh, he would forget. Good God did he forget, but still it never left him.

Then again it did.

It left him speechless. It left him awestruck. It left him dazed. Touched. For the rest of his life he would be different. Odd. He would never be like so many of the other boys. They would be able to choose "normal" lives when they got older, deciding who and what to *be*. But to Little Dougie the question about what one was going to "be" never made sense.

Unless, of course, it was about magic.

Because of that one moment. That One Perfect Moment that seemed to stretch out to Forever. That Emperor moment enchanted Dougie and held him spellbound, touched, until…until…

The crowd's clapping was a slap in time. It startled Dougie out of his reverie. Back he came. Back into the church hall.

One magic act out of a thousand could only hope to work its wonder on a child such as did that evening's performance. It was a powerful intoxicant to Little Dougie Whitestone. A woman sawed in half suddenly healed! Playing cards that disappeared into nowhere only to appear again at the loud bang of a starter pistol! Rabbits that were mysteriously created in, and then eased out of, black satin tophats! Canes that were turned into bouquets and thirsty newspaper-cones that drank entire quarts of milk at a time!

Then, the finale. The grand finale! The magic of all magic!

The music hushed. The lights gradually dimmed. The place became a silent dream.

Nighthawk slithered to the front of the stage. The Spectacular Nighthawk was about to live up to his name.

He leaned forward.

A couple in the front row threw their arms up to catch him, as he appeared to be falling directly into their faces.

But he didn't fall.

Instead, as his feet left the stage, he seemed to hit an invisible cushion. His muscular body leveled off and then, to the amazement of the wide-eyed spectators, he did it: he actually began to fly!

Nighthawk cruised silently over the stunned crowd. He moved slowly with the grace of an experienced aviator as he glided from the stage, swooshing no more than a foot above Little Dougie's head.

"Whoa!" little Dougie murmured as the incredible, awe-inspiring venture through the air took place.

"Whoa!"

Nighthawk's cape brushed Dougie's gaping eyes shut for a split second before he gently and quietly circled back to his center stage landing strip.

Even Jeremy was impressed – unable to detect any chicanery with his keen and sober eye.

The ovation was a thunderstorm; every single person was standing and cheering as the evening closed and Sherwood B. Nighthawk and the beautiful Monica disappeared behind the crushed velvet curtain.

"Angel dreams" whispered little Dougie's mom as she tucked the sheets beneath his tiny and tired body.

"G'night Mom" Dougie whispered. "Oh, Mom, did I tell you what I want for Christmas? Did I tell you huh? I want the 'Sneaky Pete Magic Show' Mom. Be sure to tell Santa Mom…"

He had been telling her for at least two months, but she patiently replied: "Oh honey, Christmas is still a month away. You just go to sleep now, okay?" But time was something completely meaningless to Dougie, who was still muttering as he trailed off to sleep and dream…

*I can fly too,* Little Dougie thought to himself, and that night he dreamed of becoming a magician.

And he dreamed of flying.

But the dreams were so real…so real…so real…

# CHAPTER IV: *ALMOST CHRISTMAS*

The morning sun had already been smiling on Deerfield Township for three hours as winter had arrived in typical midwestern fashion: practically overnight.

Before they knew it, Jeremy and Rosie were in the car's front seat, the boys in the back, making their way into the country to cut down their first "real" Christmas tree in three years.

Rosie said she was sick of vacuuming up pine needles every year and so they bought a plastic one at the Kresge store in "downtown" Deerfield.

Jeremy hated the tree.

And he relentlessly informed his dear Rosie every year about his opinion.

"Fake trees don't have that fresh-cut pine scent. And they *look* fake. And they *are* fake! And ... 'blah blah blah' was all Rosie could hear.

Finally Rosie got Jeremy to agree to not only vacuum the carpet for the entire month of January, but for the coming year as well. With that agreement solidly clarified, they were off to the Happy Holidays Christmas Tree Farm in Hamburg, the small rural village where Jeremy grew up.

Dougie was smiling as he stared out the foggy back seat window, doodling pictures of Christmas angels and rocket ships with his fingertips. He loved rides through the country. When he was a toddler, he used to enjoy sleeping on the floor of the back seat, but now he was too big for that.

The passing trees were punctuated by glimpses of roadsigns and underlined by the meandering white stripe at the shoulder of the road.

As soon as they arrived at the Christmas tree farm, the boys exited the car like panicked patrons fleeing a burning movie theatre. The work of cutting the tree was summarily left to Jeremy and Rosie.

Tad wandered through the neat rows of pine while Dougie's love of exploration drove him into the nearby woods where things were truly wild. Wild meant exciting to him: the thrill of the unexpected.

And he was about to get a taste of it too.

He went deeper and deeper into the woods when a single dead tree trunk with a girth of about five inches caught his interest. Dougie mindlessly decided to shake it as hard as he could to see if it would come down.

Unfortunately, only the top four-and-a-half feet did.

The substantial wooden teacher came thwacking down on the crown of his head, rendering him unconscious for a few black seconds. Immediately thereafter the thoroughly embarrassed young explorer scampered back to the safe haven of the man-made forest that sheltered his familiar tribe. Dougie never told anyone about it. On the way home, while the family sang Christmas carols, Dougie secretly massaged his new goose egg. *Why did God let that happen?* Questions like that frequently crossed Dougies' mind but he was, by this time, more afraid of the answer than just looking stupid.

Before he figured it all out, a shift of attention would save him. He peered out the window to see a sunset that was a spectacular ball of fire melting into a sheet of frozen, sparkling whiteness that stretched across the fields of winter.

More magic. A whole world of it. Everywhere he looked. *But sometimes it hurts to be here.*

The family stopped to eat breakfast at a restaurant, a relatively rare luxury but one that they all truly enjoyed. Whenever Jeremy coughed up the money for such an event, he went all out. "Don't even look at the right side of the menu" he would hearten, even though his kids never did in the first place.

Once home, it was time to set the tree up, which Jeremy did with the utmost efficiency. Following the customary ritual of gathering together dusty boxes from the attic, untangling strings of lights and rediscovering how fragile ornaments made of paper-thin glass should be handled, it was time to turn on the Yuletide tree.

By dusk the tree was blazing with a multitude of brightly colored bulbs, though it enshrined but a small portion of the huge collection of ornaments Rosie had gathered over the years. She insisted the tree not be "glooped up" – her term for overdone. So there was no popcorn string, no silver tinsel, and, under no circumstances whatsoever definitely none of that crummy-looking fake snow.

Her love of counterfeit trees and abhorrence of phony snow was really no big mystery. The whole family – especially Jeremy - knew that Rosie actually liked real trees better than the plastic ones, but no one wanted to suggest such a thing. Else, where would be the drama for the Whitestone clan?

Besides, the boys were far too excited about the possibilities for the quickly approaching morning of mornings, the day of days, *the* date with the angel of abundance known as Christmas Day! So why get caught up in all that fuss?

Another day was passing as a starlit winter evening eased its way into the Whitestone world. It would be pretty much like every night for the next four weeks: the routine would be the same. Little Dougie and Tad would not-so-quietly endure the agony of yet another Advent ritual at the dining room table. There, in the middle of the beautiful oaken table sat a small wreath with four candles, one for each week of "the coming." Three of the candles were violet; they represented the need to repent and have one's sins forgiven in order to be "worthy" to receive the Savior. The candle for the third week was rose-colored, to signify the joy that the season was supposed to bring.

Rosie knew about the rose-colored candle because her mother, whose name was Rosemary, had told her that somehow in the midst of all that "sin stuff" was God's truth that we're just here to have a good time. She said her mother told her that God really didn't care what we did, but like any good parent, just wanted us to play nice and not get hurt.

Rosie smiled at the thought, unorthodox though it might be.

Jeremy would eloquently proclaim readings from the Bible as this was supposed to be a reverential time for this little group of Catholics. But Rosie would sit with one eye shut and the other vigilantly open to monitor their progeny for unseemly behavior. At the eagerly anticipated end of the solemn ceremony, the kids would leap to their feet as Jeremy would gingerly remove a long-playing, seventy-eight record from a cardboard sleeve and spin it on the turntable for a listen of Bing Crosby's rendition of "The Little Drummer Boy." The boys would merrily dance, demanding in no uncertain terms the undivided attention of their audience with shouts of "Look at me Mom! Look at me Dad!" Some nights they would drink a little warm wassail, eat a little apple pandowdy and look out the window at the falling snow. After the boys were tucked in and sleeping like little cherubs, Jeremy and Rosie would snuggle on the couch until they were ready for sleep. Or, on occasion, a little hanky-panky.

## CHAPTER V: *CHRISTMAS EVE*

The kitchen wall in the Whitestone home held the only thing that mattered to two young boys: the clock. Funny how meaningful time had become. Nevertheless, the timepiece's stubborn little hands had finally made their circular journey the required number of times: it was the night before Christmas and in classic fashion, the Whitestone family was preparing for the arrival of Saint Nick.

Tad and little Dougie were as agitated as bees in a disturbed hive, roughhousing and tripping over each other in good-natured fun. Jeremy and Rosie were cleaning the dinner plates that had just been used for the annual feast that featured Rosie's relished clove-dotted ham. It disappeared almost as quickly as the sweet potatoes. Peas and beans went untouched. Milk glasses sat half-finished and smeared with the telltale signs that human young had been wolfing down their food a little too fast.

Casey, their unusually large German Shepherd, seemed to be smiling in the corner of the family room near the crackling fireplace. If only the rest of the neighborhood could see Casey this way, for he had earned a reputation as a fearsome beast if for no other reason than peeing on the next-door neighbors' poodle.

As soon as the dishes were done, all the Whitestones bundled up for their traditional game of snow-tag in the back yard. Snow-tag is like regular tag, except all of the players are expected to confine themselves to a track during the sport.

Jeremy began the happy task of tracing out the course.

First he made a huge rectangle around the perimeter of the yard, rounding out the corners as he shuffled his boots along the ground. He was careful to keep his feet close together to make a clean, narrow path. Then the course was made more complicated as he created a maze of intriguing detail. A path here, jutting out just close enough to another track so that someone might be able to reach across and tag another player. A short connector there, that could be a trap in a deceptively innocent looking loop-de-loop, and a sinisterly disguised dead end, sure to cunningly ambush some unsuspecting eight-year-old doomed to become "it."

Rosie, Tad and little Dougie watched in fascination as the child in Jeremy came bubbling to the surface, obscuring the adult "Dad" in him. They chuckled secretly as they noticed his habit of absent-mindedly sticking his tongue out as he concentrated intently upon his playful chore.

At last he announced that the course was ready and the game was about to begin. But first they had to throw fingers to see who would be "it."

As usual, it was Jeremy. The kids had figured out a long time ago how Jeremy rigged the throwing of the fingers so he would be "it" first, but they always pretended not to know. They feigned the same sort of ignorance when he would repeat for the umpteenth time a favorite story – usually a story about World War II. They had become quite the professional little actors, making it seem as if they had truly never heard the tale before.

Jeremy was pretty sure of himself. If he liked it, he liked it. And if he liked telling it by God, he wasn't going to let a story like *that* go unfinished.

The Whitestones were, for now, a happy family. They frolicked in divine white powder, playing this raucous game of snow tag until eleven thirty – when by decree of family tradition, they were coerced to stop. Mom and dad herded the boys inside to drink some of Rosie's delicious hot cocoa and then they ushered the little ones to bed. It was a family mandate that all little people be in bed before midnight, since the stroke of that hour would *be* the beginning of Christmas day and God only knows exactly when that busy fellow Santa Claus might be coming to their house.

Little Dougie and Tad both fidgeted and squirmed uneasily under their blankets.

"I can't sleep" Tad whispered in his now changing voice.

"I can't either" responded Dougie.

"Let's play rocket ships!" chirped Tad.

"Okay, you get the tacks."

It was proof, pure and simple that the Divine exists: this game of rocket ships that the Whitestone boys played. While Tad was scrounging for tacks, Dougie sat on his pillow, facing the built-in shelf at the head of his bed. Each bed was in its own niche; a design dreamed up by Rosie and built by a carpenter. There, above the shelf was an electrical outlet for a reading lamp.

Naturally, the lamp's plug only occupied one of the two outlets. That made the other one available for "rocket ships."

Rocket ships was played by wearing a pretend space helmet, sitting in the cockpit made of a pillow seat, an instrument panel that appeared to be a bookshelf with reading lamp and a plug that yearned for the insertion of thumb tacks.

Now, if one was very lucky, a thumbtack could be placed in the left slot of the plug without fanfare. But when that second tack was plugged in, it needed to be lightly inserted, then quickly released in order to create sufficient fireworks to launch the rocket ship in a flurry of ecstatic sparks that would have sent both of their parents into cardiac arrest.

Yes, Divinity exists.

The boys played until they fell exhausted into their goose down pillows and dreamed of presents under the tree.

Dougie imagined himself a magician; he wanted to do magic more than anything. He could hardly wait to open that one special, magical gift. His pestering for the last three months would no doubt ensure his procurement of it. "Be sure to mention that I want the Sneaky Pete

Magic Show to Santa"; the plea had become one of Dougie's mantras. And just in case …he had made it a point to pray extra hard each night for *all* his dead relatives. Sometimes during the rest of the year he would forget about the ones he didn't like so much. This altruistic inclusion he hoped would guarantee a "yes" to his incessant plea that he receive the "Sneaky Pete Magic Show" *this* Christmas.

Dougie dreamed that night of magic as if an angel were dreaming it for him. He dreamed of sawing women in half and putting them together again with a swoop of his magic wand. He dreamed of making things disappear and reappear and yes, magic of magic – he dreamed of flying.

In fact, this dream was so vivid, so real, that it would be years before he would even speak of it. If indeed it was a dream at all.

That Christmas eve, as he lay sleeping, Dougie felt himself roll up into a seated position, then he gently rocked to his left and far to his right, far enough to fall off the bed. But, instead of thunking to the floor, he rolled onto an invisible bed of air. He was flying! Really flying!

He was but three feet over the floor, gliding along with a surprising ease; breathless exhilaration filled his soul while he navigated over the tiles of the upstairs bedroom floor. He never noticed before how many beautiful colors his Mom had chosen or the way tiny bits of tar remained between the enchanting tiles. He hovered at the top of the stairs, flew down, circled the dining room once, and then went through the kitchen and into the basement – totally unafraid! He went 'round and 'round the basement pole, until he catapulted himself back up the stairs, through the kitchen and the dining room and into the living room.

The ecstasy of flight had somehow obscured his normal boyish desires, so it never even crossed his mind to peek at his presents. Instead, he slowed his flight until he was barely moving at all, relishing the way the light played the room. The lights on the tree were still aglow. The room was softly being cascaded with the shine of a treetop angel tenderly blinking on and off. She was emanating a gentle illumination and a comforting rhythm that seemed to echo the very presence of heaven.

Dougie towered there, motionless, timeless. Perfectly peaceful.

Then with a move of his arms, he swooshed around and flew back upstairs, where he hovered momentarily over his bed. He looked down on himself, then effortlessly rejoined his still-sleeping eight-year-old body and proceeded to slumber with the angels of his imagination.

# CHAPTER VI: *CHRISTMAS!*

It was still dark outside when Dougie awoke.

*It's Christmas!*

The thought projected with such intensity that he was unsure if he had said it aloud or not. He tossed aside his sheets and tore through his blanket as he leapt barefoot to the floor. His exuberance barred him from noticing how the winter's night had made the tiles cold. He rustled to Tad's bedside and shook him violently whilst shouting "It's Christmas Tad! Get up! Get up!"

And with that he bounded downstairs into the living room.

Once again he barely noticed the tree or the presents below. He sprang onto the red couch that stretched in front of the living room window, slamming his little chest into the cushiony velvet backrest. His eyes were like saucers, alertly drinking in the sight that lay before him. The porchlight mingled with the rising sun's barely visible rays. This morning, this Christmas morning was *obviously* very special. It had snowed overnight and large, soft, slinky flakes of crystalline perfection still parachuted to earth, adding yet another layer of beauty to the mound of unsurpassed whiteness that blanketed everything in sight. The bushes strained to hold the fluffy covering aloft while the bare-naked trees stood at attention, making a proud display of their newest artistic raiment. The lawns and sidewalks had joined as one, the snowy powder having so beautifully erased the seeming separation between cement and greenery, between wood and leaf.

Dougie was thoroughly mesmerized by the awesome splendor of it all. In his trance he remembered flying.

He remembered God.

He remembered what Real Magic was.

Then he remembered presents!

"Presents!" he loudly whispered as he spun around, catching his ankle on one of the Christmas stockings pinned to the couch's cushion. He fell headlong into the shag carpet that smelled like Casey's fur and, no doubt, had a fair quantity of that canine's coat mixed in with the fabric of the floor's covering.

He jerked himself up onto his hands and knees and swiftly trotted to the base of the Christmas tree – that favorite place of investigation – and began greedily shaking the presents in his pile.

One after the other, sheepishly glancing from side to side as he did so, Little Dougie probed and prodded the presents to ascertain their contents.

*Aha!* he thought as his hungry fingers clutched a sizable box. It was wrapped in dark blue paper that sported an array of golden stars and crescent moons that seemed to shine like the sun.

*This must be it! I knew it! This has got to be my Sneaky Pete Magic Show! I knew it! I knew it! I knew it! God! Thank you! Thank you! Thank you! You are too cool!*

*Oh man, I can't wait!* he thought almost out loud.

*No, I've got to wait. No, I can't. Yes! No! Yes!*

With that, Little Dougie sprang to his feet and bolted across the living room. He nearly trampled his brother Tad who was now standing in the living room still rubbing his Christmas morning eyes awake.

Little Dougie blasted open the door with a deafening explosion. Were it not for the fact that Jeremy and Rosie were up until three o'clock in the morning wrapping presents, placing them in piles beneath the tree and making sure that Santa's cookies and milk disappeared from the front porch, they surely would have been jolted awake by the ruckus. Dougie flew into Rosie's bed, hammering one knee into her lower abdomen and the other deep into the mattress immediately next to her left hip.

"Oomph" Rosie's mouth blew out an aching stream of air.

"Get up! Get up Mom! It's Christmas. It's Christmas and Santa's been here!"

"Hey! That hurts!" Jeremy grunted as Tad pulled a similar stunt on him – though it was his groin that caught the brunt of Tad's flying knee drop.

Jeremy shouted: "Fifteen more minutes. Then we'll get up. But if you kids can't stay quiet for *at least* fifteen minutes then there'll be no Christmas in this house!"

The boys knew better. They knew their dad to be a shrewd bargainer. They had watched in awe for many years as Jeremy hemmed and hawed incessantly, refusing to pay full price for just about anything. He had gotten deals on everything from automobiles and houses to Christmas trees and Thanksgiving turkeys.

"No Dad," they chimed in unison, "That's forever! Five minutes!"

They had become bargainers in their own right.

"Ten and that's final!" Chimed in Rosie. Whenever she said, "that's final" it was, and everybody knew it.

The boys reluctantly left the bedroom in silence, carefully noting the *exact* time on the parental alarm clock – the official time in the Whitestone house.

"Five-forty-two" whispered Dougie to Tad who quietly nodded in agreement as they silently exited the room.

For ten of the longest minutes of their lives, the boys sat cross-legged, side by side in front of the tree – the real tree.

The tree. There was something about that tree...

Dougie's mind took him away.

He was suddenly transported to another place – to another tree.

He saw a grown man, running along in a pair of what appeared to be tennis shoes of some sort; though they were nothing like the Black Batman Converse All Stars that he sported daily. The shoes looked like spaceman boots to Dougie, yet they were clearly made of white leather and white rubber. He had never seen anything like it.

Dougie watched as this grown-up man ran down a dusty dirt road on a summer's day between two perfectly straight rows of hundred-foot-tall pine trees. As the man jogged along, he gently lifted from the ground and began to glide, he was jogging in midair! At first a couple of inches, but then several feet off the dusty trail.

The man looked familiar, but Dougie couldn't be sure... as he strained his eyes he realized it was himself he was seeing, only all grown up. *So this is me some day, and I'll be able to fly!*

"It's five-fifty-two!"

Tads' shout interrupted Dougie's thinking and startled him into awareness.

"All r-r-right!" The joy-filled squeal issued from Dougie's straining larynx as they repeated the earlier invasion of the parental bedroom.

"Okay, we're coming!" moaned Rosie, "but don't you boys open anything until your dad gets his camera set up."

Jeremy was a camera nut. A maven of movies. A zealot for making sure each moment of every single Christmas was captured on film.

As the morning coffee brewed and the boys fidgeted impatiently about the living room, Jeremy set up his Hollywood-like studio. Thousand-watt light bulbs cradled tightly in silver reflectors were carefully mounted atop their stands. Electric wires threaded the furniture like a fine Oriental rug while the trusty old eight-millimeter Kodak was battened down upon its tri-legged perch.

Everyone that knew him suspected Jeremy harbored a secret desire to be a famous movie producer, and they were right. He knew he wasn't living up to his capablilities and that he was missing it. But he was like so many others: afraid and unable to give up who he was, in order to embrace what he might become. Clinging to his known self created a life of silent frustration for Jeremy: he remained a businessman. A good one, but a businessman nonetheless. Most of the time, there was no dream and precious little magic.

Nevertheless, he had his moments. And this was one of them.

By the time he was ready, the place looked like the military had descended on this little home in Deerfield Township to establish a biohazard quarantine. A piercing ultra-white light washed the room as Jeremy peered through the camera's viewfinder and gave a directorial wave of his hand; it was the final okay to begin.

The boys wasted no time.

They clawed.

They ripped.

They excoriated their gifts like rabid monkeys after juicy bananas. Bows were sent flying and ribbons were gnawed to shreds as the carpet disappeared beneath a flood of Christmas paper.

Yet there was method to the madness. At least for Dougie.

*Tad is such a clod,* he thought to himself. *He always goes for the best present first. But I know that saving the best for last is the only way to do it.*

So he set aside the blue box with the golden stars and crescent moons and proceeded to pulverize the rest of his pile.

Dougie opened a box from his Aunt Judy first.

*Yecch! I'll bet it's those stupid slipper-socks she makes. God, why doesn't she get a life?* he thought with a short-lived disdain. *I hate those stupid things.*

Next he pulled the wrapping off a brown three-foot long rectangular box. He reached inside and out came a red fire truck with a white ladder, a functional fire bell and the name "Tonka" embossed on the door. Then a box with a logo sporting a squat little top-hatted man with tails and an uplifted cane appeared from beneath a coat of old newspaper comics.

"Monopoly!" Dougie shrieked in happy surprise.

He loved to play board games. There was something about the way they could just move you into a different world, something very appealing.

One after another, Dougie's gift pile shrank until finally it was time.

*Now* Dougie mused *we shall see...Oh God, I hope...I hope...* as his fingers scratched away. First went the bow. Then the ribbon. Finally the wrapping paper gave way as he held his eyes tightly shut, then sprang them open.

"Yes! Yes! Yes!" Dougie gleefully howled, ripping away the package's shrink-wrap as he soaked in the moment.

Ah, what a moment! To have one's desires fulfilled. To drink in the gift that has been sought and finally attained. How sweet! Oh yes, how sweet!

"I got it! I got it! I got it!"

Dougie went on squealing as Jeremy contentedly sipped his coffee and Rosie quietly hummed "White Christmas." Neither of them had even begun to open their presents. Christmas had truly become about giving for the two of them. Not that they minded getting presents; that was thoroughly enjoyable too, especially when the gifts were clear displays of affection and caring. But they enjoyed the kids' faces so much that it had become the only real reason for all the fuss anyway.

At this moment, Dougie Whitestone's face became a poster child for Christmas commerce. Adorning the now unwrapped box, emblazoned in bold blue letters on top of a glaring red background were the words "Sneaky Pete Magic Show!!!"

Dougie's respiration ceased momentarily.

His jittery fingers tugged at the tight-fitting lid and carefully opened the package. There it was: the gift of dreams, the present of a lifetime. His whole universe was in a box. Nothing else existed. All this in a container not much bigger than the pillow he slept on every night.

Dougie purposefully breathed in as much air as his little lungs would absorb while he laid aside the lid to reveal a potpourri of gadgetry, a splendid assortment of multi-colored items that baffled the imagination. The central figure in this majestic array was a black box with a set of hinged purple doors that opened from the middle. The door's lintel sported a peculiar encryption with a shiny red jewel punctuating the center. Next to the mysterious box lay a deck of cards, some of which were half-sized and some a third the height of normal playing cards. There was a plastic figure of a woman in brightly-colored garb with a miniature metal saw nestled in next to her belted waist. A curious green ball was housed in a clear plastic box with a host of other magic stuff: handkerchiefs, flowers, a pop-up top hat and an instruction booklet.

Dougie sat lotus-legged on the floor for the next hour and a half; studying the manual and practicing tricks.

Finally he was ready! He was ready to begin living his dream!

But not until tomorrow.

Because the rest of the day would be spent opening still more gifts over at Mimi and Papa's houses. Those were the names the kids used for both sets of grandparents since both "Mimis" decided they were much too young to be called "Grandma." The kids just loved the fact that every year there were actually three separate Christmases.

The day finally ended and the entire Whitestone family slept like kittens in a sunny window.

Except for Dougie. He stayed awake thinking about the night he saw Sherwood B. Nighthawk and how some day, some day, he would be the world's greatest magician.

## CHAPTER VII: *THE NEXT DAY*

The day after Christmas was always an "iffy" proposition for the kids in the Whitestone family.

Some years it meant sitting around the fireplace warming with hot cocoa after a lazy morning of everyone walking around like zombies in pajamas. Other years it meant snapping to attention and getting to work like grunts in the army corps of engineers.

This year the day after Christmas was quiet. Dougie arose at six o'clock in the morning to a still peace that filled the air of every room in the house. His Mom and Dad remained in bed until almost noon, enjoying their time off work by snuggling under their comfy blankets and newly laundered percale sheets.

Tad was still asleep too when Little Dougie awoke. He didn't know it at first but he was about to spend the next six hours alone with his Sneaky Pete Magic Show discovering the secrets of the trade.

He began by once again prying off the lid. He pulled out the six inch high black box with the purple doors and the mysterious encryption on top. Investigation only baffled him, so, mystified entirely, Dougie turned to the book of directions. After more than a few moments of reading and putting part "a" into slot "b" and Part "c" into holes "d" "e" and "f", Little Dougie Whitestone beheld the disappearance box in its entirety. The instructions told him that as long as he made sure the double doors were shut, his audience would never catch on to the fact that the objects he dropped into the top hatch were actually falling behind mirrors cleverly angled to give the appearance of an empty box.

Next came the five-inch long beautiful assistants doll. She was pretty, but plastic. And the "saw" that "cut her in half" looked more like a hairpin that a real blade. Somehow a set of spring-metal clips held the beautiful assistant's torso to her bottom to give just enough room for the saw to "pass through," making it look as if she was being sawn in half.

Then there were the "sleight-of-hand" tricks that comprised the rest of the set. The clear plastic box when held just so, looked the same upside down as it did right side up. Beside the half-sized and third-sized cards, there was a deck that was cleverly marked with a system that relied on a simple knowledge of the analog clock's face. Some blue dots were faintly whited out to reveal the card's value on the back while others would disclose suit and relative location if the deck was "falsely shuffled." Another deck was subtly tapered, making a behind-the-back "blind" retrieval of some unsuspecting audience member's card possible.

It all looked just like magic.

Dougie studied all morning and all afternoon. Then he proceeded to persuade Jeremy and Rosie and even Tad to attend his first-ever magic show. A colorful crayon poster announced to all that "the World's Greatest Magician" would be performing that evening at eight o'clock sharp in the family room.

Dougie had everything carefully set up for his big debut by six-thirty, but only after wolfing down his mom's famous southern fried chicken and black-eyed-pea dinner.

The guests began to arrive. A small table covered with a black cloth held the objects that would astound them all. He darkened the room and stealthily whisked onto the "stage," which was actually the slate in front of the fireplace. His classy white gloves accented his top hat, cape, and black walnut cane. Rosie noticed that they appeared to be identical to her best set of dress gloves but bit her tongue as "The World's Greatest Magician" began.

One trick after another went as smooth as silk. Not a single faux pas. Not a glitch. Dougie was a natural. And he knew it. At show's end, he lapped up the applause like a thirsty camel.

Even Tad was impressed.

Tad. That weasel-eyed, snake-skinned, double-fisted bully that was foisted upon Dougie as an older brother was actually clapping.

*God,* Dougie thought to himself, *I love this!*

That was the day Little Dougie Whitestone decided to be a "professional" magician. That was the day he first felt the need to be a "success." Yes, he was now bound and determined to become what he had announced to the universe: "The World's Greatest Magician."

He could see it. There was no question about it. He would get there.

But something else happened that day, something much deeper than a kid getting his requisite parental kudos and winning the sibling rivalry game.

Something subtle had occurred, so understated in fact, that it passed practically unnoticed.

But Dougie could feel it. He had felt the shift before, the second time he went through the "Sneaky Pete" box, but he was afraid to admit it to himself.

Somehow in all the excitement created by his moment in the spotlight, the Real Magic began to wane, ever so slightly. The smokescreen of applause and the enticement of so-called success obscured the fact that these were just tricks, mere parlor games.

So the desire to "be someone" began to drag him away from that which was inside that needed no praise, no outer acclamation. An ingenious process was now underway. Soon, in mastering illusion, the master would fall prey to illusion.

The snow fell outside without fanfare. The beauty and wonder of a brand new world now escaped the eye of the young, new magician.

The magician was becoming invisible.

But the snow kept falling.

## Chapter vii.5

Hi. It's me again. You remember? Juriel...?

Is this ringing a bell? Yeah, I'm the 'angel' who started telling you this story.

Okay then. Now I told you that I wouldn't interrupt unless it was imperative, and that moment has come. I just want to let you know that things are going to get a bit dark for a while. I know that this has been pretty light for the most part, but I'm sure that by now you've figured out that things are going to change for our Dougie

But I'm a little concerned about you. I don't want your own darkness to overwhelm you with negative emotion...but hey, if it does, you can handle it right?

Just to let you know, we're watching and yes, we are helping you to do the things that you cannot yet do for yourself.

So, off I go now...sorry for the break, but it seemed inevitable.

Well, it must have been, for it just happened, yes?

## CHAPTER VIII: *SPLINTERING*

At the age of fourteen, Dougie graduated from Our Lady of the Stars elementary school. After a summer that involved doing little more than goofing around with his friends, he found himself in another Catholic school: a Jesuit "college prep" school. They called it an academy, a "prestigious all-boys secondary academy."

The school was filled with genius types for the most part, but they were still pretty much ordinary guys. And all of them, in their own way, were on the "golden track." Most knew what they wanted to do. Dentists and doctors and lawyers in the making, mostly in the image of their parents.

Dougie thought he knew what he wanted to be too, and he did well academically, but found his talent for things magical left him a bit of an outcast. His friends grew tired, and eventually annoyed, at the fact that all he ever wanted to do was show them his latest card trick.

Meanwhile, the school was playing its' own bit of chicanery on Dougie and his classmates. Little by little, the priests and scholastics, and even the lay teachers at his school not only taught them *how* to think, but *what* to think. They reinforced what Dougie had learned at Our lady of the Stars grade school, while they were professedly teaching him how to think on his own. It wasn't done maliciously, this delicate brainwashing. It was simply that they too had psyches that had been thoroughly scrubbed by the dogma of Mother Church. There were a few notable exceptions, of course. But even they couldn't help it. Well-intentioned though they were, they were bound by their roles.

Black robes speak for themselves.

He had been taught how to think about God. So it logically followed, since God made all things, that Dougie saw the world colored with the same tint, brushed with the same hue.

Apprehension slowly and clandestinely replaced the joy he had known so well in his childhood; the joy that had been based upon his childlike ability to experience himself as one with all that is. Before long he carried the common man's consciousness of separation.

A hidden fear had become, without warning, the foundation of his thought system. Everything was suspect. One needed to be cautious, to be careful, on guard. A subtle defensiveness, attack in disguise, permeated the atmosphere he lived in.

God, and therefore everything else, was, in the end, to be feared.

No one seemed to be able to explain, at least to Dougie's satisfaction, how it was that one was to love this frequently angry God who may, or may not, let you off the hook. No one took seriously his assertion that both could not be done at the same time.

As a result, he, like so many others raised in his religion, simply went back and forth: fearing God one moment and then loving him the next. And, of course, God was always a "him."

In his gut he knew that God was not such a villain, but listening to sermon after sermon, priest after priest, and every now and then a bishop or two, Dougie unconsciously relinquished his intuitive awareness for the doctrine of the group.

*After all,* he reasoned, *how could all of them be wrong and I right? They're grownups. What do I know? Besides, they've been doing this for two thousand years!*

Nevertheless, he wondered. He questioned, but the answers were always lacking. He disputed but was "put in his place" time and time again, until he lost his will to challenge authority. So he stopped wondering, at least aloud.

On top of that there was the shame.

Oh dear God the shame.

It started very early on, even before he could talk. A dirty look for a dirty diaper. A scowl for talking too much or, good heavens, for playing too loud. Then came the formal reprimands, scoldings for crying too tumultuously and lectures for laughing too boisterously. And there were the spankings. Always on the naked skin of the rear end and always in the name of goodness.

Spare the rod and all of that.

At the tender age of one-and-a-half he made the mistake of walking in on one of Rosie's bridge club events. He came in there naked to show everybody how proud he was of a new body part he had just discovered.

His mother gasped and leapt from her seat and covered up his genitals and hustled him off to his room.

The message was clear: not okay to be sexual.

And, of course, they never talked about it again.

Until the night Jeremy had "the talk" with the boys. He took Tad and Dougie for a drive late one night and told them about the wonders of procreation, the sacred nature of the sex act and the necessity of remaining chaste for fear of falling into "mortal" sin.

Mortal sin was the biggie of the biggies. It was a sure ticket to eternal torment. Sex was the one thing that would get you to hell faster than a speeding bullet. Most of the drive that night Dougie was nodding off to sleep in the back seat while Tad and Jeremy were mumbling something about wet dreams.

So, between the nuns and the priests, the teachers and the principals, not to mention the parents and grandparents, aunts and uncles, Dougie didn't have even a small chance. Again the message was clear: it was pretty much not okay to be Dougie.

He even had to hide his magic, because after a while the whole family got sick of it and let him know in no uncertain terms.

He learned it well: don't talk, don't trust, and, whatever you do, do not, under any circumstances, feel.

By the time he started to date at age sixteen, he'd already had a two year long relationship with the only thing he felt he could really trust: alcohol. He used to steal it from his parent's liquor cabinet. They always had enough on hand so that they never even noticed when a little bit disappeared. Yes, here was something that made him feel whole, no matter how splintered he had become trying to please all those people and be what they wanted.

Losing touch.

He only had one girlfriend throughout his high school career, and she ended up breaking his heart.

Her name was Sherry.

He met her during a game of Ping-Pong in Sherry's basement. At the time, she was Tommy's girlfriend. But Sherry liked what she saw in Dougie and started flirting with him from the start. She batted her thick lashes at him, but he hardly noticed. Not because she wasn't beautiful, but because she was. She had big, deep blue eyes and long, thick blonde hair. Her svelte figure was any sixteen-year-old boy's dream. She was not only drop-dead gorgeous but smart and fun to be around. Unfortunately Dougie had it wired that nobody much cared for him and that, for sure, someone that pretty wouldn't see much in him. But Sherry knew what she wanted. Finally, she flat-out told him that she was hot for him and boom! He fell like water over Niagara. Head over heels in love, he spent his entire high school career thinking about her and planned on marrying her one day.

But time moved on and the two were separated by some of the unexpected twists of life.

After his graduation from high school, the lure of the tropics swayed Dougie to leave Sherry for a summer. He returned to the news that Ted Parker, one of his "best friends," had taken advantage of his absence and cold-heartedly moved in to taste some of Sherry's sweetness. Dougie listened slack-jawed one hot August evening as he heard the news dribble from Sherry's own lips.

He simply shattered.

He spent the next two days in a semi-catatonic state lying on the beach with a bunch of strangers. He could only stir enough energy to go to the bathroom now and again, but other than that he lay motionless and face down in a beach towel quietly sobbing.

Later it all turned into rage and a bout of fisticuffs with Ted. That battle ended in a draw. There's nothing worse than a draw for a teenage boy defending his honor. A good beating would have been better, if nothing else but for the sympathy.

The depth of his bitterness was such that he found a sick consolation in a failed suicide attempt by Sherry. He was actually disappointed when he heard that the weapon she had used on her self was a coke bottle cap. Clearly it was not so much a genuine attempt as it was an adolescent gesture whose meaning eluded Dougie.

By the time he got to college, the neuronal pathways were well entrenched. He was in for a four-year drone of an old tune: school work all week, get drunk, maybe get lucky on the weekends and start all over.

Losing touch some more.

After college Dougie got married, but not to Sherry.

He married a young lass named Betty that he met shortly after his mom died. As it turned out, Rosie had been doing a considerable bit of drinking herself. She died at the age of fifty-one, right on Dougie's birthday.

His marriage to Betty lasted nearly ten years, but she too had been raised on the drug of approval, so it was destined not to last. The relationship deteriorated over time, with the help of lots of alcohol and lots of anger. Dougie was so engrossed in his career that he was rarely home, and when he was, they did little more than fight.

The whole thing ended in a bitter divorce.

## CHAPTER IX: GROWN UP?

Dougie Whitestone was now forty-four years old, and he was, literally, "the World's Greatest Magician."

His fame rested largely on his talent for making objects of any size "morph" into something else: an eighteen-wheel truck turned into an elephant, a twelve-story building into a pea in a thimble, a cruise liner into a laughing dolphin. It was all done with mirrors and smoke; only these were expensive and eccentric, modern-day techno-wizard versions thereof. It was the "Sneaky Pete" show for grown-ups.

He had mastered his craft and toured Europe and Asia, where he received accolades in such abundance that they were bested only by the exorbitant fees he could easily demand. His prominence swelled at the same breakneck speed his fortune did. South American and Australian audiences had granted him such a reputation for his amazing act that he had earned stature roughly equivalent to royalty, but with three times the wealth. He had been on radio and television more often than the nightly news and had gone through just as many relationships.

Tonight he was going through just as much Irish whiskey.

Halfway through a fifth of Jameson, Dougie slouched into the arms of a well-upholstered, high-backed chair that ensconced the end of a twenty-eight-foot dining room table. Well-polished black walnut.

An enormous crystal chandelier tinkled above, cascading prisms of color about the room.

The magician's mind raced backward in time.

Dougie was once again thinking about Sherwood B. Nighthawk. He had gotten the news a month ago that his friend had died. They had become close during his magician's apprenticeship. Sherwood kept Dougie in touch with his experiences of the paranormal: séances and tarot readings, spells and conjurings and the like. And the coup de grâce, his own mentoring from an enlightened Master from the East.

Sherwoods' background closely paralleled Dougies', in that he had grown up with parents who were religiously orthodox and so passed on a heap of guilt and shame to their son. They were nice people and there were great times, but that wasn't enough either. Somehow he found his way to the mystical tradition within that faith and there he found respite of sorts. But it too, like so many Western religions, was little more than an intellectually based exercise. There was some understanding of the body and the emotions, and some understanding of the energetic body. But there was no scientific approach as to *what to do* with a human being as an energy field. Questions about who and what human beings are were answered in many entirely accurate ways, but without a practice, without usable tools that led to experience beyond the physical, it wasn't enough. Sherwoods' magic couldn't get off the ground until he knew.

His knowing came when he encountered his Master. He only met him once. He made it all so clear with just a few words: "I am more *you* than *you* are right now. You are *deva satva*, Divine but not yet. You will feel it when I arrive within you."

Then the master touched Nighthawk's "third eye," his ajna chakra, the Yogis call it. A trance ensued and when Sherwood came out of it several hours later, he could no longer tell the difference between himself and the sky, between himself and the trees or the rocks, between himself and all of it. After a while it became an ongoing experience for Sherwood.

When Dougie asked, what that was like he was told: "It was like the sun coming up for the first time."

From that point on, the 'magic' was natural for Sherwood. He learned to be like a child most of the time. When he needed information he could easily access it by emptying himself and simply allowing it in.

*This way of being is not something that can be taught, but it is something that can be transmitted.*

Dougie got the message.

Young Whitestone learned an initial lesson from one of his mentors' own early experiences. It was Sherwood's first séance and he was the epitome of skepticism. A group of about eight individuals were there and most of them were interested in contacting a lost loved one. But not Sherwood. He was there to find out if there was any truth to all of this stuff.

They were all holding hands with eyes closed as the leader of the group began to talk and moan. Something about "There's not enough energy here. They're trying to contact us, but they can't because there's just not enough …"

"At that moment," Sherwood informed his novice, "there was someone walking outside the plate glass window. As this man ambled by, the window began to shake, and as it did, the twelve-foot-long solid oak table rose off the ground, shook for about a minute, and then gently landed back on the floor."

Dougie was impressed, but not as much as he was with what happened next. "I stayed in the room after everyone left. I climbed underneath the table, pushing it off the floor with my back to see if there where hydraulics or wires anywhere. There was nothing. If this guy got this table up off the floor with some sort of mechanical trick, I know I would have found it. I even inserted a mirror under the legs and felt around with my finger to see if anything was inside the legs. Nothing. I checked the glass too: not a thing."

This taught Dougie exactly what he needed to learn. "It's not only okay," the Famous Flying Magician would say, "but it's *important* to be skeptical, to question. Don't accept anything just because somebody says so. Find out for yourself, for therein conviction, and ultimately, knowing, lies. And once you know, don't forget."

Over the years, Sherwood sent tomes of reports from other séances he attended. The content of these papers thoroughly intrigued the young apprentice. Things like seven different levels of universes and a god called Wyta, who was purportedly in charge of the spiritual universes while other deities were in charge of things physical. There were beings all over the place it seemed. Some of the dead who died prematurely were apparently more apt to be seen easily because their energies were still intact. People who died from more 'natural' causes and whose energies were more dissolved were less likely to be seen as they merged with the All. Or not.

In the end, there was a deluge of information, and much of it was impossible to prove or disprove. Sherwood understood that things spiritual might or might not be opposed to things religious. So he shared with Dougie his deep desire for not only understanding things, but for making them real. In fact, Sherwood would often say, "It's all about *you* Dougie…it's all about *your* self-real-I-zation."

But then, somewhere near the midpoint of the apprenticeship, tragedy struck.

In the middle of the night about five years before, Dougie got a call that left him stupefied: Monica, Sherwood's wife, had been found murdered in their house.

Sherwood came home from the store one day to find that she had been strangled to death by some freak serial killer. To double up the horror, she had been carrying their first child. They eventually caught the man and went to trial. In the middle of the proceedings, Sherwood actually told his wife's murderer that he forgave him, right there in the middle of the courtroom. Still, he was sentenced to death. Then one night while he was just lying in bed, the famous flying magician, Sherwood B. Nighthawk, took his final flight and left his own body for good.

  The shock of the entire affair had totally embittered Dougie; his thoughts became a foul stream of pain.

  What little respect he had left for "God" turned to venom. At Sherwood's funeral, Dougie went out into the parking lot; his brain half-way-hammered from too much alcohol, looked up at the stars and gave "God" the finger.

  "Why didn't you take me instead?" he slobbered. "You fool!" he snarled. "He was the only man I knew who could do real magic! I only do cheap parlor tricks and you know it! You big jerk! Why in the name of Hades didn't you take me instead? You fumbling idiot! You call yourself God?"

A plethora of curses ensued until Dougie ended up a fetal mass of thumb-sucking jelly on the asphalt from whence he eventually had to be lifted and taxied home.

Tonight he was in a similar state as his semi-stewed mind turned to Sherry. "How could she have jilted me?" he queried in an ever-deepening self-pity. He remembered her suicidal gesture with the bottle cap. "Hardly a real try" his resentful mind clattered as he recalled his disappointment at her weapon of choice. "Damn it all anyway, my Dad was right. You can't live with 'em, and you can't live without 'em. Freaking women! Sooner or later they leave and when they do, they take you for everything you're worth if they can. Leave you with half a heart in the process…walk out the friggin' door and take the hinges to boot…"

So, here was Dougie, still lost in his past. He had wealth but couldn't enjoy it. He had fame but all it did was drive him into isolation. He had good looks but all that did was help him start shallow relationships that typically perdured on par with the longevity of a mayfly's love life.

The famous Whitestone had now polished off the entire bottle of Irish. It was just about all his body could take, but it was nowhere near enough to quiet his chattering mind. He stumbled up the long winding staircase that led to a hallway of doors. In his stupor he wasn't sure which one was the master bedroom. Somehow he found it, leaned into it and tumbled like a rodeo clown into the thick mattress.

But he didn't stay there.

After fifteen minutes of watching the room spin like a figure skater, he managed with a great heave to lift himself into a seated position where he teetered on the edge of the bed. From there he rocked until gravity gave him the catalyst that sent him headlong into the bathroom door. The low tone of a dense thud resonated throughout the room as the World's Greatest Magician slammed himself into solid wood with a ferocity that would have killed a man with a thinner skull. The blow rendered him unconscious. He lay motionless on the floor for the next three hours while a small cut in his forehead produced two tiny pools of blood that managed to coagulate over the slits of his drunken eyes.

When he awoke, he thought he'd gone blind and began to scream. He rose from the floor in so much agitation he clobbered his head into the bedpost and knocked himself out once again. When he reawakened, he repeated the whole affair with the exception that this time he managed to paw away the dried up blood before giving himself another concussion.

Afraid, embarrassed and still drunk, Dougie crawled across seventeen feet of Italian quarry tile to hug his commode. Upon his arrival he lunged his head into the water and vomited something resembling split-pea soup in rhythmic heaves of abdominal gut-wrench.

Ten minutes later, he was staring at a medicine cabinet full of amber-colored cylinders with his name on every one. Valium. Morphine. Methaqualone. Lithium. Secanol. Tuonol. His M.D. would have made Elvis jealous. There was even some heroin in there from some guy he'd met in Mexico. Enough drugs to kill a small army.

He stared.

He thought.

He stared some more.

He reached for the Valium but ended up with the morphine. He swallowed twelve of the little white tablets. It made him real sick, but that's all.

The next morning, he awoke to the strains of Mahler's Resurrection blaring from some unknown source. When he finally recognized that the offending noise was coming from his radio alarm, he smashed it with a clenched backhand. The clock fell silent, but the incessant, droning tape in his head didn't. There they were again, those thoughts, running through his profligate, pathetic mind:

*Never again.*
*I'll never do it again.*
*I'm swearin' off the bottle this time for sure.*
*Yeah. Right.*

Dougie's drinking was seriously out of control; it was to the point where "never again" really meant "until tonight."

Oh, he could quit. He proved that enough times. When his willpower was really tweaked he could go a good long while. But then his over-eating would kick into high gear. Or his over-sexing. Or his over-working. Or all three. He could quit for months that way, even years. But sooner or later, he always came back to the juice.

It was killing him and he knew it.

He just didn't care.

He knew that too.

He didn't care because he was washed up. He noticed quite some time ago that his hands were considerably slower. A little boy in the crowd last Saturday night caught him sleeving a card – a novice move that even rank amateurs could pull off.

And the week before that he had hammered some guy's wristwatch beyond recognition and had to buy him a new one.

That wasn't the hard part. The hard part was the embarrassment, the shame. He used to laugh it off and joke it away, but in those days it was inexperience, not self-loathing that was to blame.

He was losing and he knew it.

And he didn't know how to keep it from happening, to keep it all from slipping away.

That night Dougie Whitestone went to bed early after downing another fifth of Irish.

## CHAPTER X: GOODBYE

The sun's eager light beamed across the room's undulating air. Birds sang out in the well-treed courtyard as the *kerboink kadush* of the gurgling stream ran down the side of the mountain that was one of many on the Whitestone estate.

But none of that mattered to the little boy who was drying up inside of the famous magician's adult body.

Dougie groaned himself out of bed with a curious grin of satisfaction ornamenting his face. He looked peaceful. His dream during the night was most curious.

He had been running down the street of his youth in metal baseball spikes when a large menacing crowd formed at the end of the block. An obese and grotesque woman was smoking a belching cigar and began scolding him for being late. After weaving his way through the throng he came upon a police officer who was about to arrest a magician for severing his right hand. The magician held it in his left hand, reattached it to his right wrist and disappeared through the boards of a cedar fence.

When Dougie awoke, he remembered the dream and knew exactly what he was going to do today.

The magician went down into the kitchen and started his morning ritual of coffee. He loved the stuff. Dougie pulled his cobalt-blue mug from the sink, still stained with yesterday's tonic. After the perking stopped, he slowly poured in the black brew, then added two golden teaspoons of sugar and lastly the cream. Genuine cream. Fresh. Nothing less would do and it had to be from Caulder's dairy or he wouldn't touch it.

That fact made him smile.

Something he had not done in a long, long time.

Dougie slid his cup onto a gargantuan mahogany coffee table, plopped into the fluff of an overstuffed leather sofa, scooped up his cell phone, and called his cousin Jim.

Jim was the only family member that ever really "got" Dougie. The two loved each other, plain and simple. They could go for years without communicating and as soon as they started a conversation it was as if they never stopped talking in the first place.

"So, as I was saying…"

"Dougie? Is that really you? Damn it's been too long."

Upon hearing Jim's voice everything was as if he had just come home.

"I've decided that I have too much stuff, so I want to give it all away!"

Dougie was actually laughing.

"Yeah, that's right Jim! All of it…"

Jim wasn't laughing. Besides being a cousin and a good friend, he was Dougie's attorney and always made sure he didn't screw himself. Jim had spent a number of years on the street where he learned to be a real straight shooter and he knew that Dougie's estate was now worth nearly two billion dollars. He had been there to help Dougie during those days when he didn't have a shaker with which to salt his eggs and he wasn't about to let him just toss it all away.

"What's going on with you Doug?"

"Nothing" Dougie calmly replied.

"What in blazes do you mean 'nothing'? A guy like you ought to be on top of the world right now, not talkin' a bunch of crap about givin' it all away! Listen Dougie, you've worked real hard to get what you've wanted out of life. You're a talented guy with a lot goin' on for yourself, why would you just want to give it all away? You know, very few people in this world get to do what they love for a living and even fewer make the kind of money at it that you do, so what is goin' on my friend? Why would you want to throw all of that away? You've worked your tail off getting together a great career all these years, climbed to the top of your field and boom! Just like that you want to trash it all? I know you aren't heading for a monastery or an ashram or some horse pucky like that… Hey! You're not planning on doing something stupid are you?"

Jim knew that Dougie sounded strange but really meant it when he said he'd wanted to "…give it all away."

Then the phone went dead.

Jim hit redial. All he got was voice mail. He tried for two more minutes before it dawned on him.

Then he dialed 9-1-1.

## CHAPTER XI: FLIGHT

He marched up the steep incline, his black cape rippling behind his taut neck like a flag unfurling in a blustery wind. His top hat tumbled downhill as he leaned into the whistling storm and hiked forward with the determination of a tidal wave. He propped himself on his black walnut cane and looked straight down one thousand feet.

He didn't hesitate, not even for a second.

He lunged into the jaws of the unknown.

He lurched toward the horizon for a split second, flinging his arms straight ahead as his powerful legs uncoiled. Then his mind went blank. He looked down the precipice and noticed that his sight was waning as he plunged earthward in a speeding frenzy.

Everything was fading to black.

He was losing all the feeling in his fingers and his hands. His legs and arms went numb as if he were freezing to death. There was no sense of smell or taste as the noisy rush of wind fell silent.

A pure pitch-blackness enveloped him.

Dougie was dying before he could kill himself.

# CHAPTER XII: THE VOID

Everything was moving in ultra-slow motion as the magician's midnight-black cape trailed his plummeting body.

Complete peace.

Utter serenity.

The bliss of pure nothingness permeated all.

It was over... it was all over...

Or was it?

Without warning the blackness sparkled with white.

*It's snow!* Dougie thought to himself. Once again large, soft, slinky flakes of crystalline perfection parachuted to earth. Once again pure sparkling whiteness and the possibility of novelty and newness was falling everywhere. His entire field of perception became a magical display of blinding beauty.

And peering through the thick flurry Dougie could see himself—himself as a child.

He was remembering that moment when he was a boy. That moment when he was bursting with joy on his way to serve God; that moment of moments when he crashed through the barrier of time and knew who he really was; one with all that surrounded him, with himself, with All That Is.

Suddenly there was a flash of brilliant white light! It bounced off the inner walls of his cranium; a piercing pain stabbing like an ice pick to the eye, overwhelming his consciousness.

More silence. And everything seemed to move in slow motion, in a peaceful grace.

Then a tiny, almost imperceptible sound made its way into his awareness: it was a woman's voice.

She was singing.

More like humming, kind of "ahhing" actually. The sound was captivating. Pure.

He had never heard anything like it; it was so, so…perfect.

Then something odd began to happen: the voice began to blend with another voice, then another, until there was a chorus of voices. A symphony of sound like a watery wind, like children laughing and birds warbling their morning song filled his awareness. And somehow it was happening all at once. It was the most breathtaking music he had ever heard, a wondrous melody to ears deaf but a moment before.

It was almost too beautiful.

Then the Voice spoke: "What are you doing?"

The question arrived in a soothing and quieting fashion, almost like a mother asking a child.

Dougie stammered in response:

"Wha...who...what?"

"What are you doing?"

"I don't know."

"That would be correct."

"What? What do you mean?"

"I mean you don't know what you're doing. Do you know why?"

"Why what?"

"Why you don't know what you're doing?"

"I'm sorry, this is making no sense to me."

"Indeed it makes not even a little bit of sense. But the question remains: 'Do you know why you don't know what you're doing?'"

"I ... well ... I guess not."

"Okay. Let's start there. You don't know what you're doing and you don't know why. This is actually the condition you were in when you decided to do what you did."

"I'm sorry, this is still making no sense to me."

"Okay, let me make it simple for you. I'll just tell you: you don't know what you're doing because you don't know what you are"

*Why that's ridiculous. Of course I know that ... I'm ... I'm ...* Dougie's mind wasn't giving him any help, he was drawing a serious blank.

As if reading the blanks in Dougie's mind the voice spoke again : "So, *do* you know what you *are?*"

Stumbling the words out of his mouth, Dougie strained to talk. "Why…why…I don't know…I seem to have forgotten …"

"You're not alone."

"Huh?"

"I speak of your condition. All of humanity is in this state. They have forgotten the only thing that really matters. Yet they go on living lives of utter nonsense and distraction from this truth. Some are willing to ask the question 'who am I?' but very few actually question *what* they are. And fewer still are those who have the intensity needed to actually find out.

But for now, never mind. We'll cover that later. Let's see if we can stimulate your memory a bit. Let me give you a hint about what you were doing…you jumped off a…"

"A cliff! That's it! I jumped off a cliff and killed myself! Oh God, I killed myself…I mean I…hey! Wait a second. I *tried* to kill myself! What the hell happened? Why am I still alive? Did I kill myself or not? Am I dead? Am I still alive?"

"I think the answer to that question should be obvious by now. A better query might be 'why?'"

"Why what?"

"Why did you try to kill yourself?"

"Are you kidding me? … Why? … Why? … I can't believe more people don't do it. I'll tell you why all right…how about because everything about my life sucked? That's why! I tried everything I could to find fulfillment. And *all* of it failed! Towards the end, all I could feel was this gaping, hideous wound inside myself. And, it just wouldn't go away! All the loss! I lost everyone I ever loved in one way or another! Sure, I had money and lots of things, but ultimately they meant nothing to me.

Everything failed, not a single thing worked! Even my magic! I used to love it, but when I grew up I realized there was no magic."

"Your entire world is magic."

"Phooee! You couldn't prove it by me."

"The whole gorgeous place is perfectly made, so much so that there is no need for my involvement. And still I do get involved. Yet I speak to you. I am speaking to you in words right now, but normally it is through the symbols that I speak."

"Symbols? What symbols?"

"Everything that surrounds you. I use it all. The majesty of a sunset, the song of a bird, the music in the wind. I speak to you so eloquently through the touch of a loved one, through the poetry of a waterfall, through the *magic* of a *magician*!"

"Say, who *is* this? Who am I talking to anyway?

"I'll tell you what Dougie, let's just call me 'The Voice' for now."

For some unidentified reason, this was fine with the confused Magician.

"Okay. The Voice it is."

"Do you remember the day you slid through the snow when you were a little boy. Can't you just see the beauty of that day again? Don't you recollect how pure everything was when you were that young? Don't you recall the magic that you knew as a child?"

"Well, actually, I was just revisiting that day. How did you know that?" *Oh God. I'm going insane. No. I know I'm insane. It's got to be a voice in my head. That's how he ... mmm ... she knows. But that's too logical a thought for a crazy man...or is it? How would I know? I don't know what's happening. Crap, this voice, it's right. I don't know.*

Trying to hide his puzzlement, Dougie stammered, "No. No I don't remember. I'm not a kid any more."

"That's the problem."

"What?"

"Children understand. They don't get lost in time like so-called-adults do. They just get up in the morning and start their day. No worry. No cares."

"Yeah, sure. It's that simple when you're a kid. But when you grow up, after a while, it all gets so empty. Nothing truly satisfies any more. Like me, ...ever since I lost Sherry. Mahogany furniture...Ferraris...teak trimmed sailboats...giant homes...nothing worked. Nothing could ever replace the...the..."

"The love?"

"Yeah, that's it. The love. What happened to the love? You know, every lover I had seemed perfect at first. Then, as time went on, the glow would fade. Next thing you know, we would start seeing each other's faults and end up fighting or, worse yet, feeling practically nothing for each other and taking each other for granted. Next thing you know, it would end.

And if that weren't enough, finally, I found one…one! One that seemed perfect practically the whole time. I never saw anything wrong with her. In a delightfully strange way it was as if I was looking at her through a screen door, and the screen held her flaws. But I was never interested in doing anything but seeing what was on the other side. I was always looking through it to see the…the…the *reality* of her. It was as if I had been given brand new eyes with which to see her. I never saw anyone else that way! Everything she did just tickled me. I think I was truly in love with someone for the first time in my life. And not only that, I liked her too! She was smart as a whip, beautiful inside and out, and loaded with wisdom too! And – now get this — she accepted *me* and loved *me* just the way I was! Finally, for once, I didn't have to *change* myself for someone! And, we could have such fun together! God, we could joke and laugh for hours about anything! It was like we were in a bubble whenever we were together and all the world was perfect…her and me! Ooo, God, the sex, it was off the charts! Ecstatic and spiritual! Half the time I felt like I *was* her!"

"That's because you were."

"Huh?"

"And are."

"Who cares? I lost her. It hurt. I was miserable."

"How can you lose what is everything?"

"I don't see the point you're making."

"You will. You cannot move the mountain of bliss."

"What does *that* mean?"

"In time. Let's take another track. The problem was a result of what you were pursuing. You were pursuing your happiness."

"Of course I was pursuing my happiness. What's wrong with that?"

"Nothing at all. It's just that happiness isn't something to pursue. And it's no big accomplishment."

"What? Are you kidding? I spent my whole life seeking happiness. Sometimes I found it too! Most of the time, there was some kind of backlash. Some negative side effect, do you know what I mean?"

"As a matter of fact I do. Still, it was your *pursuing* that was the problem. Happiness is simply something you *came* with. This is why I am asking you to remember being a child. When you were a child, you were just bursting with joy weren't you?"

"Well, yes, I guess so."

"And then, somebody came along and made you unhappy, yes? Your parents, your brothers, your grandparents, the priests, the nuns, the other kids, the teachers…"

"Okay! Yes! That's what happened, I know all that, but that's no help, just knowing my childhood traumas hasn't made it all go away!"

"No, but what has made it stay with you is the way you have reversed the equation."

"What? I don't understand?"

"Sure. Someone else made you unhappy. Now you expect someone else to make you happy. Or some thing, or some condition in your life. You did this instead of finding it directly. You've been routing your happiness through the bottle, through the pills and the expensive cars, and, mostly through relationships, but none of it has worked.

Let me ask you Dougie, isn't it about time you found your happiness directly, through your own nature?"

"Through my nature?"

"Yes, through your natural state, your boundless state, as it was when you were a child, only better!"

"Yeah. Sure."

"Please Dougie, don't be so quick to assume that this is absurd. Your resistance to being duped is so ironic. Already you are duping yourself by acting so small, as if all you are is a body, a mind and a set of emotions. I assure you, you are much, much more than that alone."

"How do you know that?"

"Because right now *I am more you than you are*, that's how."

"What's that supposed to mean? And who the hell *are* you anyhow? You seem really familiar but I can't put my finger on it."

Dougie thought to himself: *This must be one of those memory things again. For sure I'm going insane. No. Now I know it for sure, I'm insane. It's got to be a voice in my head.*

"What would the difference be?"

"See, you read my mind. You've got to be a voice in my head."

With that Dougie inserted one index finger in each ear and began blubbering a series of 'la-la-las' to make the Voice stop. But it didn't. He could still hear the next question:

"If I am telling you the truth, and you *are* boundless, and you *are* One with All That Is, and you *are* much bigger than you think, what would that mean? What if you are, right now, not only hearing the Voice of the Divine, but you are yourself Divine?"

There was a long pause, as Dougie was suddenly speechless as well as thoughtless. It was as if he could no longer muster up the energy to fight the onslaught of something that seemed way too good to be true.

The Voice went on:

"What if the greatest thing in the realm of all possibilities was in fact, the truth? What if you were being offered something greater than anything you've ever been able to imagine? Would you be able to accept it, or would you 'resist being duped?' "

After another pause of several minutes, the 'Worlds Greatest' feebly replied: "Gee, I don't know."

"And once again, you would be correct. For to accept this, the Greatest of All Truths, that there can be but One, that all separation is simply illusory, requires the dissolution of the *you* that you think you are. It means your personality needs to be dissolved."

Yet another pause.

"Isn't it obvious Dougie? If there is a God, who by definition is All There Is, then all there is must be a part of this Divinity?"

"Well, that *does* make sense. *If* there is a God… You know, you feel so comfortable to talk to, like I could tell you anything and you wouldn't judge me. On the other hand, I feel so inadequate…"

"That would be because, right now, what you are being *is* inadequate."

"You know, some of the stuff you say is pretty weird."

"It's just a matter of time before you see how 'weird' Dougie. But what is truly weird is the world that *you* have made. A world of pain and suffering. And all of that suffering has come as a result of this separation that could never happen."

What do you mean 'world that *I* made?' *I* didn't make this world. You did. Or something did. Or, whatever!"

"No Dougie, this world that you see *is* of your own making. First you judge things as you would have them be. Then you *see* things as you would have them be, or, in other words, what you have judged them to be. As long as you use your intelligence in this way, you are bound to see the same old thing every day.

Even this conversation is a good example. Conversation requires concepts. Concepts require contrast. And contrast denies the truth."

"Hmm. Okay, I think I see what you're saying. But you still haven't told me who you are."

"I'll tell you what Dougie, let's just keep calling me The Voice for now. And let's stay focused on what it is I am doing."

"Yeah, okay. What are you trying to do? What is this all about? As far as I can tell this is doing nothing more than confusing me."

"Good."

"It doesn't feel 'good' to me."

"That's because you're such an expert."

"An expert? At what."

"You think you're the expert of yourself. You think you know yourself better than anyone does. Isn't that true?"

"Well, of course."

"Do you know how many cells are in your body?"

"A lot."

"Do you know, or not?"

"No."

"Your body has two-hundred-trillion nine-hundred-billion eight-hundred-ninety–three-million six-hundred-seventy-two-thousand three-hundred and six cells at this moment. It also houses some one-hundred-fifty-trillion microbes that aren't even human."

"Do you know how many of those are brain cells?"

"To be honest, no."

"Sixty billion one hundred million three hundred and thirty six."

"Whoa, what are you, Rain Man?"

"So you don't even know your own body, yet every day you get up, seeking the fulfillment of 'your' desires, based upon the *illusion* that you *do* know your self. This is just a stupid way to live. You see Dougie, there is something that this life is longing for, it is not a desire, it is its destination. The only choice we have is whether or not we go towards our destination. It is the way we handle the process that makes the difference. Not just changing the objects of desire.

Now let me point out, there is a reason you came into such a form. There is a reason for this kind of intelligence. And it is not just reproducing, or making money, or forming unstable relationships with others of your species."

"What then?"

"To remember. But simple knowing will never be enough to bring about true conviction."

"What will then?"

"Only experience. Once you have experienced your Self as something beyond the body, beyond the mind, and beyond the emotions, will you know. Truly know."

"But then how can I truly know without the experience? And since I haven't yet had this experience, I can't really know? Is that what you're saying?"

"Something like that."

"Well then, there's no way out. This feels just like when I tried to kill myself, and apparently I have failed even at that! This really blows!"

"You have a problem, that's all."

"Oh God, I Sure do!"

"Fortunately, I have a solution."

"You do?"

"I have powers beyond your imagining and I am going to explain something to you. Your body is like a rocket ship."

*Oh god, there I go again. I'm hallucinating. Now I have a little kid's voice going off in my head.*

"No really Dougie. You see, this whole thing, the whole nine yards, has been fashioned very carefully. Your body – of which you admittedly know very little – has been crafted in such a way as to function as an escape vehicle, if you will, from the experience of being so small. You have heard of the Masters?"

"What are you talking about? You mean yogis and shamans and stuff like that?"

"Precisely."

"Yes, my mentor had a guru. So what about them?"

"They know the secrets of the body. They know how to use the body itself as this 'rocket ship.' The 'rocket ship' takes off when specific, precise circuits are closed. Just touching your index finger to the tip of your thumb, for example, sets off a kind of an explosion between your ears that in turn alters your perception.

99

Your perception, of course, determines everything else, including how much 'here' you feel versus how much 'there.'"

"Here versus there?"

"Yes Dougie. Isn't that the basic problem, that you feel like a prisoner? Do you not experience yourself as a hostage of fear? As a tiny little creature born to live as the slave of a body that suffers pain and eventually decays, and dies? As a pawn of a mind that you cannot control and the casualty of an array of emotions that fill you with terror and dread and sorrow and yet more fear?"

"That's *exactly* how it is inside for me!"

"I know."

"You *do* know, don't you?"

"Yes, and I also know that it isn't that way for you *all* the time. There are also many times when you're feeling fantastic and loving and like all is well with the world. Isn't it also that way for you?"

"Yes, just like a roller coaster. One minute I can feel so…*divine*, and the next so…so…much like a slug!"

"That would be due to your dualistic nature. You *are* divine and animal. What you call your human nature is just the flux between the two. Once you reconcile your self – or should I say selves – to that fact, things will begin to disturb you less.

In fact, this is how the Masters work," the Voice went on, "they know how to form a gap between you and your mind, between you and your emotions, between you and your body. And they have the secrets of the energies: how to stabilize and lock them so your mind becomes a wonderful tool, your body becomes an ecstatic place to live, and your emotions no longer overwhelm you with that which is painful. Instead they become only what makes life juicy and delicious, if you so choose. And once those energies are locked, bliss becomes a permanent state."

"Well that doesn't seem to help me much right now. I threw myself off a cliff and right now for all I know I am about a millisecond away from splatting on a rock! I don't know if this, that I am experiencing now, is still a body or not."

"Correct again. So here's what I am prepared to do for you: I am going to free you."

"Free me? From what?"

"From your self. Your 'small s' self."

"From my self? What are you talking about?"

"As I said you experience three natures. One is animal, the other is divine. But what you call your 'human' nature is really just a vacillation back and forth between the two. The animal is securely in place. So is the divine. But the 'human' isn't. It is however, a certain kind of freedom. So now that you have attained this human form, you may become anything that you want. You have earned this freedom, but you are suffering from it now because you lack awareness. Once awareness is gained, this freedom becomes your joy. But for now you and the rest of humanity are suffering from this freedom."

"I'm not sure I know what you mean by 'awareness.' I think of myself as 'aware' but I don't see that it brings me this great freedom or joy that you seem to be talking about."

"Indeed, the kind of awareness of which I speak is, quite literally, another state of being altogether. It is actually being in another dimension and knowing it. Awareness is not something you do. If fact, the less you do, the more aware you become. The less your activity *inside* becomes, and this inner activity is what you call 'me'…the less your personality becomes … the more aware you become.

Don't forget this Dougie, awareness is not something you *do*, life *is* awareness… not just something to do. Too many have become human doings instead of human beings."

As if a light bulb were going off, Dougie exclaimed: "Hey! Wait! Are you talking about something like that moment when I was a kid? When it felt like I slipped through some kind of wormhole or something? Because time seemed to stand still and – I guess that would be beingness – and everything was suddenly right with the world?"

"Yes Dougie. Like that. Time *did* stand still for you that day. It's *all* a matter of time."

"Okay, now it feels like we're actually making some sense of all of this. Tell me about time."

"When I said 'it is a matter of time', I was burying a treasure for you. I was stating, in as few words as possible, a grand, magnificent, and unfortunately esoteric, truth. It is a truth that is now available to you.

So, when I say it is a matter of time, I mean it. It is time – or, to put it more accurately, your *sense* of time – and therefore space – that has you trapped.

No time, no matter. No matter, no time. Some of your scientists in the early part of the last century saw this truth and uncovered it as a time-space continuum."

"You're talking about Einstein? I didn't get that when I took it in school, and I still don't get it. What are you trying to say?"

"I'm telling you, except for 'now,' there is no time."

"Hmm…let me think about that for a second." Dougie stroked his chin quizzically. "No, it seems to me that there's got to be such a thing as time. I remember a past, there's this moment now, and there's a future out there somewhere I'm sure. That's time isn't it?"

"Yes … and … no. Allow me to put it to you this way and let me ask you a question, okay?"

"Fire away," said Dougie, feeling a sweet kind of anticipation.

" The past, is it over?"

"Well, it's over of course."

"Then it cannot exist. Do you see that?"

"Okay, that makes sense."

"And the future, has it occurred?"

"Well, no, not yet."

"Then it too is not in existence, it has not yet occurred, yes?"

"Yes."

"Therefore, there is nothing but this moment, correct?"

"Well, I guess that *is* logical." *Something's wrong here. This sounds like bull to me.* There was a churning in Dougie's gut that he couldn't quite put his finger on

"And yet there is a chatter in your mind at this moment that wants to deny this and cling to the way things have been, yes?"

"Yes. And a feeling in my gut…"

"Always a thought brings up a feeling. But let's stay on task here.

So if this moment is all there is, there is no time, except for this moment. That is all the 'time' there is Dougie. The past is over and the future is not yet. A moment comes into existence, we have it, then it is destroyed and the next moment comes. It too is quickly destroyed. Some of your religions have deities that do this destroying, but too often this aspect of Divinity is thoroughly misunderstood. Imagine how maddening existence would be without this flow. Kind of like the other dream states you are in."

Dougie looked puzzled.

"You know, the ones you're in at night."

"But you said 'other.'"

"Yes. By 'other' I meant to show you that the state you are in now is actually a state of sleep."

Once again puzzlement waved over Dougie's face.

"What would it be like if you suddenly found out this is all a dream?"

"A dream? Well, then I guess nothing would matter because at some point I'll wake up."

"As I said, no time, no matter. No space, no time: *nothing matters!* Good for you Dougie, I think we might be getting somewhere."

"Okay, so what? What does this have to do with me and my screwed up life?"

"Everything. Understanding the nature of this sleep is one of the many keys you have been given to assist you in finding your liberation.

So, please my friend, take a good look at it.

If nothing but this moment exists, why fret about tomorrow or brood over yesterday? It's not *thinking* about the past that is the problem, but *living* there. A major reason the lives of so many are utterly bleak is this ordinary human propensity for projecting the past upon the future. Instead you could be seeing the future as an extension of the present, where all is well."

"Yeah, but every 'present' moment isn't perfect, all isn't well. What then?"

"No Dougie, you only see it that way because of your judgment, remember, you only see things as you would have them be. Allow me to demonstrate; let's try an experiment, okay?"

"I'm not so sure about this judgment thing, but very well…experiment away."

"Can you make yourself happy right now? For one moment, do you have it in you to make yourself happy? Go ahead, try it right now."

Dougie closed his eyes and somehow, with the sheer force of will and much to his surprise, he did indeed make himself happy.

"So there you go! If you can make yourself happy for even one moment, that means you have the power to make yourself happy in all the moments. Not just the one"

"Wow! I see" muttered Dougie.

The thing about your mind is its propensity to think about what you do not want, instead of what you do want.

So do you see that it is this monkey–chatter, this self–imposed–sleep that is the source of all of your angst? Isn't what we're talking about the very type of thinking that led you to the brink of self-destruction in the first place? And is this inability to stay in the moment, in the present, *in life itself* not the real problem?"

"I guess."

"You know."

"Okay, I know."

"Exactly. At some point, you *will* wake up and then you will see the truth about your Self: *that you are boundless!*"

"I'm sorry, it doesn't seem like a dream, nor do I feel boundless for that matter."

"I know Dougie, so I am going to simply *give* you this experience, and then you will see that nothing is real."

"Oh really?" Dougie said with more than a tinge of sarcasm. "What do you mean nothing is real? I've heard that before and it sounds like bunk to me."

"No-thing is real! No *one*, single thing is real because *every*thing is *One* energy. $E=mc^2$ or, everything is One. Not two, not two billion. Only your mind has broken it all up into so many pieces that it is driving you mad.

The truth that *It is All One Thing* is what can make your dream such a happy one."

"And how is that?"

"You see Dougie, the fundamental function of the human mind is discrimination. It automatically makes a distinction between one thing and another. Try to think without, at the same time, contrasting, and you will find that you can't."

Dougie closed his eyes, and began to try to think. His mind began to conceptualize objects but he immediately realized as each image arose, it *was* in contrast to something else, even if it was a kind of blank background. And it was easy to see that 'comparing' was still contrasting but to a lesser degree. He was stunned.

"All pain comes from this fundamental act of separation. This is what I meant when I told you concepts require contrast.

No separation, no pain. All of your agony has been about 'I don't have enough,' hasn't it? I don't have enough food, sex, love, power, drink, pleasure, money or whatever! Ninety percent of the prayers I hear are just that: 'give me this, give me that, save me from this, help me with that … it's very rare to hear deep spiritual longing

– deep desire to be dissolved from one's self, from ones 'me-ness!'

The answer to all of life's difficulties comes in the *realization* of the Oneness and this comes from dissolution of the personality. It is this 'making it real' that I am about to give you."

All of a sudden, everything inside changed. Just like that, Dougie was aware of a kind of sensation, but it wasn't really a sensation at all. It was more of a moving stillness that came upon him. Unexplainably dependent on form no longer, pure consciousness took over. Truth presented itself with great lucidity:

*Whoa! This is sweet. Um, I like this, I feel like I'm in a different dimension or something. I can be, I can exist it seems, without thinking. I'm sort of looking down on, observing from a bit of a distance, my own mind. And my body, I can feel it, but somehow the sensation has within it the knowledge that it is not me. And then again, it is! God, this is most enjoyable! Ooo, I like this! I feel as if all of my problems have just vanished but I know they are still 'there.' They are simply not in this reality and yet it is a reality that somehow subsumes the other.*

The Voice gently intoned: "You have been having this experience of a different reality, I know. But in the meantime I am helping you bring it in here to the 'mundane' as you call it. And even though there is much more than you are now able to experience, I would like you to see the difference between these two states. And the possibility of bringing them together into one 'blended being.'

Because we need blended beings Dougie. We need the animal and the Divine pulling the same way to render a new kind of 'human.'

Welcome to the Silent Revolution!"

Dougie just sat there.

"So there you go Dougie. Do you now see that what you experience most of the time is a dream? It's the dream-game called your life. You were trying to end it because it became a nightmare and I don't blame you. But now you have an opportunity to change it *all*."

"How? I mean, this experience I just had, how do I get it to stay?"

"It is just like any other dream: anything here is possible. All that needs to change is … *you*! Your thinking, your feeling, your emotions. In short, your personality"

"Whoa there! That's all of me … at least so it seems! What else is there?"

"More than you can now know. But it would be foolish to give an ant a ton of gold, yes?"

"Okay, I hear you…'to give a ton of gold to an ant'… hmmph!"

"There's nothing wrong with ants Dougie. We have to stay with your honest to goodness experience. Not your fabrications. You are currently just like most people, and so, these three aspects *are* what you call your 'self'; it is all you know of yourself.

And since you are like most people, it will not be until your death bed that you realize you've spent ninety-nine percent of your life in your own mind."

"Is there no help for me then?"

"Ah, but of course. You're talking to me.

You also have a vague notion of your self as energy. At least you know when you are low on it, or high on it, and that it runs the other three?"

"Vaguely, as you say."

"The freedom I offer you is based upon, at first, a disidentification with these aspects of your self. You have just had this experience, that of 'Self' beyond the physical.

On the other hand, this dream you are having is sourced by your 'monkey mind.' This constant chattering, the incessant flow of data from your brain to you keeps you so preoccupied that you ordinarily have no faculty to experience the *real* you. And since your mind is totally preoccupied with the past, and the past is over, you are constantly living in a place that does not exist. This you now understand.

So the dreamer needs to be awake, not asleep. You must awaken to your own boundless nature and live as the beautiful, wonderful, amazing being that you really are. That brain of yours has misled you. It keeps you looking in all the wrong places. Places outside yourself. To get this Dougie, you must go within, for that is where Heaven is!"

"I've heard that before, but never really believed it."

"Indeed. Believing it would never have been enough anyway. Only experiencing it. Belief has this world in a virtual state of non-stop war. And the end of war, the end of all suffering lies not just in these great truths, but in the beings who will be able to live them, to merge with them and *become* them."

Once again Dougie was staring. He was absorbing it like a sponge.

"I understand your chagrin over what you perceive to be your loss. But all of this has been to bring you to the place where you finally admit that you don't know what you are, what anything is for or how to relate to it. It is into this truly open mind that the truth can finally be poured."

More staring.

Then Dougie stirred.

"Say, you never did tell me who you are…other than 'The Voice.' And now you're here talking about an understanding of the universe like I've never heard before…what are you, some kind of god?"

"It doesn't really matter what you call me. Call me nobody if you like. Call me nothing. No-thing. Call me everything. It's all the same, for to be no one thing is to be all things.

And so it is with you."

*With me?* Dougie thought.

"Yes, with you. You see, self-concept is the world's great preoccupation, but it is a vain effort. For it is only at the end of self-concept that the truth about Self can begin to be apprehended. Everyone is trying to put a frame around a picture and then say 'that is me.' It would be better to use the image of a kaleidoscope, for you can be anything you want and it's always changing. And then throw away the kaleidoscope for you are also the space within which the existence of the scope is possible in the first place.

Bottom line: any label will be insufficient…so let's stay with what you know, what your experience has been, okay?"

"Well, to be honest, it feels like my experience is nowhere near enough. Not even these awesome experiences I have been having with you. I'm beginning to feel what you've been talking about. I feel like I'm nothing, but I am. I am!"

Dougie was beginning to laugh again: "And yet … I don't know why … but I'm feeling so good right now … that it's fine if you're just … that I'm just … 'no thing.'

You know, the moment I heard you, I started feeling so inadequate in your presence, yet so comfortable. All of a sudden I forgot my problems, my life, hell, I forgot who I was!"

"Forgetting who you *really* are *is* hell. Forgetting your false self, letting the stranger finally walk out, this is heaven…welcome home my love!"

God, I do feel like I'm home! I feel so good! Not only that, I can feel that you're…excuse me and my concepts and my words here again …a part of me."

"That's because we are virtually indistinguishable. We are one. Truly one."

"So you're me? You're my Self?"

"You've forgotten already?"

"Oh yeah. How could I forget?"

"You did. You forgot about 'me' too, but I never, never forgot about 'you'."

"Thank you."

"You are more than welcome my friend. By the way, I have always been there with you. I never left and I never, never, never will. I have seen your pain and suffering and I know it well, as I feel it too. And you need never feel abandoned again, not so long as you live in this body – but only if you so choose. You see Dougie, I can't stop thinking about you. When you decided to kill yourself, you had forgotten all of the miracles, all of the 'angels.' Did you think I would just leave you behind?"

"Yes. I did think that."

"This is the genius of absolute love.

What I do is set this up so you can have all that you've ever wanted and in that way free you to go on to something even better. But the plan involves no need for pain, only in the seeing that all that is on this plane is really about nothing. Nothing, that is, except for you. You are the only thing that matters here, because you are the only thing that is real, for you are the embodiment of love.

So go for it. It's all yours. Don't be afraid to live. That's what you're here for. Be prepared for the time of your life Dougie Whitestone. Everything you've ever wanted is on its way to you now, and so you shall have it until you want it no more. Then you will come back to your Self in delight. Repression and the illusion of separation from me are things of the past, and, of course, the past no longer exists.

So go! Run! Run fast and sure and fly with the eagles, for now you truly have some understanding of life. Accept all that comes your way with glee and let it pass through you without holding on. This will make it a thrill ride so divine and perfect and pleasing to every aspect of yourself that you will be amazed and you will fall in love with me, your Self, the Ruler of the Universe, once more. This is what brings you into my peace and within this peace is everlasting life. You shall experience yourself as so much more than you could ever have imagined. Do not take this lightly, but take it as your life's purpose, for you really did come here to save the world. I have told you many times before that I am always with you. I meant just that. I meant that you and I are One and that we cannot be separated. I am in your brothers and your sisters as well. And not just some of them, but all of them. And all of us, together, are One as well.

So choose whatever you want here, have no fear of reprisal for I have no judgment about what you prefer. I only want what's best for you. I only want what you want for you."

"And what is that? What do I want? I really don't know."

"What you really want the most is the truth, the simple key that will open up the door to your ultimate fulfillment. You have been given that key, and it is the secret of seeing the inevitability of the now. I will never say anything more important than this:

This moment is inevitable; it can be no other way.
This moment is inevitable; it can be no other way.
This moment is inevitable; it can be no other way.
So live in it as if it were *all* that is, for it is.

It is ironic, is it not that the key to escaping the pain of life is just living it?

Use it and you needn't fret about what you perceive as your lack. I have called you to *mastery —the greatest goal of all!*

The rest, your magic, your dreams, your love, your sex —I have heard all—will flow like water. Like a beautiful stream of love will time be for you *my love*. My gentle one, my fierce warrior for whom I have the highest regard. *My very self.* How could I not love you – you! My dear one, my love of loves –you, my flowering ray of sunshine –forever have I loved you and forever more.

Dougie's thoughts were singing: *Now is forever…I Am here…I am here now…I am loved here! I Know that I Am and can simply be, just simply be!*

A cloud of sweet, blissful communion descended upon them and a deep Oneness replaced every fear, every question being answered before it could be asked.

So 'they' just sat.

For a long time, they just sat.

# CHAPTER XIII: MAGIC FLIGHT

Dougie was suddenly flying.

He looked down to see a set of talons at the end of feathery legs. . *Am I dreaming? Who cares, this feels fantastic!*

He was surprised to notice that they moved when he moved his legs. *My God I'm a bird.*

"Not just any bird my old friend. A hawk."

The masculine voice was familiar, but only vaguely.

Dougie gasped as he turned his head to his left and saw something flying alongside. It was another hawk, only it bore a man's face, the very familiar face of Sherwood B. Nighthawk, the famous flying magician.

"I showed you that magic was real. Now you shall know that all that is, is magic."

With that Nighthawk swooped towards the ground. Dougie was immediately pulled into the wake of the flying magician by some unseen magnetic force.

And with that came a chaotic tumbling at breakneck speed.

*All right, I can so this!* Dougie thought.

And with that Dougie was flying confidently aside his skilled guide. They swooped and barrel rolled, they did stalls and landings, loop de loops and accelerated falls followed by daring pullouts. Dougie was truly enjoying himself. He was smiling from ear to ear and laughing like a kid again. *Wow! I am seeing everything differently, just like 'the Voice' said.*

The pair landed in a sumptuous giant oak that sprouted up from a verdant park. The tree provided a sturdy branch, a perch from which to observe as people strolled below. It was a perfectly warm summer day.

A man below who sported a beatific smile looked straight up at Dougie. His transmission and somehow his voice could be heard very distinctly even though his mouth didn't move.

*Welcome Dougie. Isn't it a gorgeous day?*

Mysteriously he felt as giggly as a child with a toy and answered in his mind: *Sure is!*

*I couldn't agree more* Nighthawk intervened without speaking.

*Telepathic and televisual communication is the norm here. I am sure you will enjoy much of what you shall see and hear Dougie,* the man on the ground 'said.'

Dougie was noticing people's faces and how they all looked so young. He also noticed that everyone was beautiful without necessarily having attractive features.

*Beauty really is in the eye of the beholder, Dougie. It is an inner matter, not an outer one, as nearly everyone on earth believes. There is practically none of the judgment that comes from simply seeing a body.*

"What is the name of this place Nighthawk?"

Shifting from telepathic to verbal communication was as easy as people taking turns pushing each other on playground swings.

"This is called Nasus Elak. It is a stellar grade seven planet. The place is filled with those who came from earth, but only those who reached a certain level of spiritual development. Those who, in their last earth incarnation, came to experience their Oneness with the Divine on a permanent basis before they left their bodies are allowed to come here. You are currently the only exception, but you are only visiting."

Dougie wondered if they had to worry about things.

*No. There is very little digression from pure love-thought on the entire planet. When a digression occurs, the thinker feels intense pain and nearly always immediately changes his or her thought.*

*We eat food that we create from 'blueprints' that are held in the ether and summoned at will by the inhabitants. Our houses are built by pure thought-energy so there are never problems with payments or anything like that.*

Then Nighthawk laughed. There was a mysterious kind of feeling whenever someone laughed on Nasus Elak. Dougie couldn't put his finger on it; all he knew was that he felt giddy and childlike each time one of the inhabitants chortled because it made him laugh too.

"In fact," Nighthawk continued, "there is no such thing as money here. There is a fundamental desirelessness in the hearts of all, filling them with bliss.

In addition to that, there is the very clear understanding that there is always enough, and that is what makes it so. The populace of Nasus Elak knows that all are but One Self anyway. When I give to you I give to myself. Conversely, were I to take from you, I would only be taking from myself. Thus there is no war or poverty or crime and no need for teaching morals.

There is no such thing as disease either, as all realized before they left earth that they could heal themselves. And that was in the gross physical plane where healing by 'supernatural' means went very much against the grain of the groupthink. Here it is much easier because all it takes is giving *in* to peer pressure, not fighting *against* it."

He laughed again, seeming quite amused with himself.

While he was musing over what Nighthawk was telling him, Dougie noticed something that startled him so, he had to blink a couple of times and turn away and blink again, as if to say he couldn't believe his eyes.

A beautiful blonde-haired, blue-eyed girl walked below.

"Sherry!" exclaimed Dougie. "My God she looks just like she did when she was seventeen! No, better!"

"Well . . . " Nighthawk started but didn't finish because at that moment flashes of light appeared and softly surrounded the girl's body until she emerged as an eagle and sped to a nearby branch where she gently landed.

Dougie became slack-jawed.

The eagle sent a televisual; Dougie watched a movie play in his mind as clear as if it were on a theater screen.

In super fast motion he saw Sherry being born, then the movie backed up and he saw her evolve in reverse: first an infant, then a fetus, then an embryo. At that point Dougie saw a laser beam of pure white light back out of the embryo. The light beam reversed like a shot through space until it reached a strange turquoise-colored planet.

As the beam entered the planet's cloud-free atmosphere, so did Dougie; he marveled at the view. Mountain peaks sported trees that literally glowed in an incredible light show of translucent amber and red, blistering blue and yellow. Tree trunks of cyan and rose, some shimmering as though made of glittering white marble were scattered across the landscape. Dazzling teal and white leaves nestled roses that hid fruit of such rare beauty that it defied the imagination. The movie showed people walking up to orange trees and picking off pears while children rode wheel-less bicycles that floated over the soft petaled ground.

Then the televisual made a surprising shift.

Suddenly the light beam was coming directly at Dougie as he instantly found himself perched back in the tree on Nasus Elak. The light veered to his right and suddenly where the eagle had been, there sat Sherry in her full womanly glory.

She spoke.

But as she did so, he felt his own body morphing back into his youthful human form.

"Hello Doug. Long time no see." Dougie remembered that she was the only one who ever called him Doug.

Wishing he were seventeen again, Dougie nearly toppled off the branch as his body had transformed from hawk to seventeen-year-old adolescent human.

"How'd you do that?" The words stumbled from his mouth.

"The same way you just did. It's the way things have always worked. We just forgot; and now we're remembering."

Sherry winked as Dougie thought about his conversation with 'the Voice' and what was said about remembering. He also thought about the part when the voice spoke of one's animal nature, because he was imagining making love to her.

*Minds have to agree though Doug.*

With that Sherry lighted from the branch and floated in front of Dougie who found himself panting.

Her body moved closer and closer until the voltage nearly caused him to faint.

*Hold on my love. I know what you think, but this is even better.*

She kept moving nearer even though it appeared as if she could come no closer. He was losing his breath but she kept coming. He closed his eyes and began to feel as if he was losing himself in a rapturous delight.

She was melding with him. They were in a seventh heaven. Their bodies became one. And then she *passed right through* him!

Dougie squealed from the ecstasy. They had reached paradise.

Then she did it again from the other direction. He was going ballistic now.

Then, suddenly it was over and a glorious state of extreme bliss ensued.

Sherry resumed her explanation while Dougie vainly tried to understand what had just happened. He felt completely satisfied yet felt no desire to "have" Sherry again.

"Doug. Doug. Dougie Whitestone" Sherry's voice was calling.

"Huh?" Dougie mumbled. "This is like the stuff 'the Voice' was talking about…" His voice trailed off, trying to keep secret the dialogue, but Sherry gave him a knowing and approving smile before she went on.

"You know, people have already decided what they're going to see, before they see it. It's called judgment."

"That's nonsense" chortled Dougie, still enjoying his rapture and not yet ready for anything intellectual.

"That's right" Sherry calmly replied. "Nevertheless, the experience you are having now is challenging all of those preconceptions of yours, yes? Here we call this your nonsense! We no longer rely on five senses like you do, so that's our non-sense."

Sherry guffawed and snorted she started laughing so loud. She hardly noticed that Dougie didn't get it and went on with a joyous, light tone in her voice:

"Our finely tuned sense of intuition allows us to perceive the matrix, as well as manipulate it for our own enjoyment at will. In addition to that, we are keenly aware of the limits on the senses, the narrowness of the band of perception that is imposed on the field. We know full well, all the time, that it is our projection that we are truly seeing, not 'reality' as your species thinks.

It's just a playground we're on Dougie. We can play better now, that's all."

Then she laughed. She smiled at Dougie in a way that only she could. *She could light up a roomful of rooms with that smile* he thought out loud.

Sherry laughed again.

So did Dougie as he allowed his ecstasy to extend into the moment.

"I'll be seeing you again Doug. But you have some decisions to make. No matter what you choose I will always love you."

To his utter astonishment as she was saying those words, her face changed into his grandmother's face.

Dougie rubbed his eyes. Then her face became a wolf man's face, then some sort of a fish-like creature.

He rubbed his eyes harder and longer.

Then she morphed into the woman who was once his wife and then it became Sherry's face again.

Somehow, this time he understood.

And somehow he knew that she was seeing his face change too.

An entire parade of faces ensued.

And somehow the pageant of faces explained so much in so little time. It came in a way that satisfied him; while the immensity of it all shivered him to the core.

Sherry began to change again. She started to glow. She grew brighter and brighter, until she had transformed into a seven-foot-tall snow-white Angel. Her well-feathered wings fluttered, stretched and groaned open to the fullness of their span. Then, all at once, she began to shrink, abruptly turning into a five-inch ball of blindingly pure, radiant golden light. The ball zipped right through Dougie's middle and sped off into a distant forest, leaving the startled young man trembling, breathless, and yet, complete. He was virtually mesmerized by the bliss.

*Not now!*

Nighthawk's transmission interrupted Dougie's trance.

*It's time for you to choose.*

Dougie tumbled from the tree, but magically floated softly to the ground.

Time ground to a halt. The trees stretched out their arms to give him shade while they dropped their petals for him to stroll in their softness. Once again he was in heaven as he ambled along. Pure unadulterated lucidity caressed his mind. The truth spoke of itself with perfect clarity: heaven is indeed a state within. Yes, sauntering in this lush place was sweet, but what was now being divulged was that what was coming *out* from him was even sweeter.

He stopped and sat. He sat still. He even stopped breathing, fully aware that he was now in a light-body, not flesh, as another mystical rapture held him aloft. The wind slowed to a whisper that whirled gently and warmly around his head and asked the question. "To be or not to be?"

Then, all of a sudden, without warning, it felt like his mind had been quietly replaced. Mysteriously the mind with which he was now thinking was brand new, yet utterly familiar. It felt so good, and at the same time as if nothing had happened. He instinctively knew that the change was fully in accord with the genuine depth of his own true will. It seemed like he had been asleep and dreaming and now he was awake, even though the state he was now awakened to was there all along. It was like he was still four years old and had just dreamed that he had been an adult. His consciousness was swimming with a peaceful ambiance, yet it was shimmering with an energized clarity. It was as if the sun had just come up for the first time.

This, Dougie thought, is *better* than magic. Immediately, as if all of the heavens agreed, Dougie knew the answer with absolute certainty. The thought reverberated with divinity. The idea charged through his mind. There was no doubt about his choice. In fact, there was an absolute certainty.

*To Be!*

*Yes! Yes! Yes! To be! To be! To be!*

With that he leapt high into the atmosphere of Nasus Elak and did a double somersault followed by an airborne, triple barrel roll before bouncing on an unseen trampoline that hurled him skywards where he began jetting around like lightning: zigging in this direction then zagging in that.

He sped towards the sun, gaining speed until he merged with the light above.

And then he was gone.

## CHAPTER XIV: I'M BACK!

So there you have it.

That's the story of Dougie Whitestone and my small role in his life.

Oh, sorry, it's me, Juriel…remember? I'm the "angel" who began this story!

I told you I wouldn't intervene, unless the Voice said it's time, in which case, it's time! That's when we act. So that's why things go the way they do. The universe always has more tricks up its sleeve than you think.

In my years as both an angel and a human being, I have noticed that the Voice is always speaking. But It usually calls a little louder during one, poignant time: when we are ready to chuck it all. When the overarching question has become 'What the hell am I clinging to anyway?' When we are ready not just to toss it or to lob it or to pitch it, but to fire it, to fling it, to hurl it all right back where it came from.

That's when you have found your own Voice.

And that's when the command is heard.

*So be not afraid... for there is nothing to fear!*

## CHAPTER XV: ONCE AGAIN.

The midnight black pupils of Little Bobby Daniels' eyes yawned. The apertures of his sapphire blue eyes gaped to drink in every bit of light that was bouncing off the spectacle that held him mesmerized.

There before him was a poster…

"Whitestone!" Bobby gasped, "Oh my God, he's coming here! He's coming here!"

**The Beginning.**

## About the Author

*Brian Black lives in the beautiful state of Michigan where he enjoys riding his motorcycle, composing and playing music, and, of course, writing.*

*In 1990 the Reverend Mr. Brian J. Black retired from active ministry in the Archdiocese of Detroit, and in 2003 he was initiated into the practice of Isha Yoga – the Yoga of the Divine - by Enlightened Master Sadhguru Jaggi Vasudev.*

*Brian is also a retired therapist, a four-time champion of the Toastmaster's International Speech contest, a gifted corporate trainer and keynote speaker, and is considering launching a new career as an actor as well.*

*He may be contacted through his website: innerskysite.com*

*Cover by Jennifer Everland at Everland design: jeverland.com*